I loved you

Chaitali Nath

They think I love you because of how handsome you are, but trust me darling, I'd
have loved you the same if I were blind and you were bald.

Acknowledgements

In the tapestry of creating "I Loved You," I find my heart brimming with gratitude for those who transformed this poetic journey into a reality. To my unwavering pillars of strength, my parents and brother, your unyielding support has been my guiding light through the maze of emotions poured onto these pages. A heartfelt thank you to Ipshita Prosad for breathing life into the collection with your artistry, shaping the cover into a visual symphony. To Tannishtha Datta, Ipsit Karmakar, Aishani Ghosh, and Abhijeet Bhattacharjee, your early readings and candid reviews have been invaluable, shaping the contours of these verses. To Siddhant, for being my confidante through it all, for hearing me out even when I knew I wasn't being sensible, and so much more. Urvashi, you are my steadfast supporter, my number one hype woman, believing in me more than I dared to believe in myself. And to Sushant, for being my everything – your presence is woven into every line. This book is not just mine; it's ours, a collective creation nurtured by the love and encouragement of these extraordinary souls.

1

My heart is broken
My soul is scarred
My voice is shaken
And the path ahead so hard

My breath is still there
And so is my heartbeat
But life isn't here
Because it's now defeat

I have a place to go to
With a lot of disbelief
That I will ever be make it through
With this huge backpack full of grief

I turn to you for comfort
But you're gone long back
And you're the reason of my discomfort
And the belief in life that I lack

I was with you through thick and thin
I was the one who fought your battles for you
And you left me hanging in
The midst of an ocean of lost love to swim through

I dreamt of a life with you
Such did I love you
But you choose not to
And left me with heartbreak to go through

2

I thought you were all I need
Until I met me
I thought I needed protection in your Love's seed
Until I became free

I felt you were the cure to all my problems
Till I met my dedication
I felt you were the proof to all my theorems
Till I discovered the facts in me

I believed your reviews were everything
Till my critics took charge
I believed my life without you had no meaning
Till I saw how my efforts made my view enlarge

I ought to thank you for believing in me
And bringing the true me out
I ought to thank you for setting me free
From so many a doubt.

3

Look at me and tell me
The truth that you hid
The truth, to know which, I'd even die
The truth you forbid.

The reason why you left me on hold on each phone call
The reason why you never called back
The reason why you refused to make eye contact, at all
The reason why you held back.

Held back the knife you were going to use on me
I don't know which crime I committed
Except that I loved thee
With all my heart and sacrificed all I wanted.

I didn't know you'd turn out to be such a devil
And break me like that
I didn't know you had a side this evil
I would've stayed away even from the shape of your hat.

Well, that's on the past
And I demand my reason
The reason why you decided to choose me for your evil blast
Of your hatred season

4

I woke up each day
For you, I needed to pray
For you to win each battle
So that you never heard failure's rattle

I stayed up late at night
To keep you away from your fright
Of darkness and quiet everywhere
I stayed up, because I care

I made sure you were well blessed
I made sure it was only love that your life caressed
I took all that pain on me
Never did I even ask for a pinch of glee

Not that I didn't like being happy
But because I liked you being happy
Because I couldn't see a single tear roll down your face
I chose that, all the troubles, I would face

I wonder where I was wrong
I wonder how a strong love that held so long
Couldn't melt your heart's ice
Couldn't make you nice

What was my fault
That rejection came to me, by default
You hated me for loving you
You despised me for caring for you

I don't think your guardian Angel is hated by you
I did more than any guardian angel would do
And yet you hate me so much
That hate could burn anything it would touch

So did my love burn away
How long would it even stay?
But I'm proud it held much longer than anything else
My love for you was something else

I don't regret it
I don't hate it
But I hate the feeling that you never knew
That my love was what was making the greatness in you

5

I waited my eternity for you
Fell in love each time I saw you
I wonder where my love fell short
For you never found me to be your sort

It was only when I walked away
Did I realize the problem was in my way
I gave myself to you, like I'd submit myself to a God
But you didn't know what to do when you're God

You thrived on my love
I prayed for only you, my dear love
Little did I see that I lost myself on the way
Only to realize that today

It does hurt, I wouldn't lie
But for you, I won't cry
For I've picked myself up and gone
But yet, this heart does feel forlorn

I wish you'd realized what I was
And how much of your success I was
It was for all my love and my prayers
That you are one of the big players

But nonetheless, I'm gone and I will be
Wouldn't look back and see
You're my past and I've buried it once and for all
Good bye to you now, once and for all.

6

Yesterday, I thought you were mine
Today, you're everything but mine
Maybe because I wasn't yours yesterday
And it's known to you that I'm yours today

It hurts to be ignored, plain and clean
Having to avoid being seen
And having to avoid seeing
Just to kill that feeling

Maybe because you were my adrenaline
And because you were my dopamine
Maybe because you felt like home
Did I build a dream castle of foam

Not to realize that you'd blow it away
So far, so very far away in just a day
I know I'm not perfect, I'm not like her
I'm not as beautiful as a peacock's feather

But that doesn't mean I'm no one
Or that I deserve to be treated like one
I'd never known vulnerability till you
I don't think adrenaline brings the rush that you do

For that poem, my first reader were you
And here, the poem is about you
I know you'll say it's a beautiful poem if I send to you
Not realizing that it was written for you, about you

7

I love it when you notice the small things
You have no clue about the feelings it brings
Even I don't know why
But near you, life seems as peaceful as a clear sky

When you smile, it's wonderful
It's after I've met you that I feel beautiful
I don't know if it's you or me
But life's started having more glee

I know you're not mine
Nor will you ever be
But to have someone who
Is just as old as new

Just as known as unknown
Just like a breeze that had flown
Past my hair, making it fly so high
Though just a moment, but it was worth a try

Someone who makes me laugh like no other
Someone who I can speak of to my mother
Someone who notices the things no one else does
Someone who does things no one else does

Someone I know to be a good human being
But more importantly, a man worthy of kneeling
Before, for you're a person I've never met another like
Always there to save us from any strike

I know for a fact that I'm safe near you
And I have said that to people very few
But you are special to me
For it's you who's brings me out of me

I'd never known me
Till I met you and found glee
I'd have never known you
But it was fate's play that we met out of the blue

Everything's been a whirlwind since then
But I don't regret what has happened since then
Because it has made me more aware of me
And it has taught me so much glee

8
Late nights
Old fights
Old woes
Paying their dues

A lot of pain underneath
A smiling face as a sheath
A broken heart hidden
Confessions forbidden

Someone to speak to
Someone to hold on to
A little courage
And a whole lot of entrapped rage

But it cools down
Eventually does dissolve the frown
But not the pain
It just gives way to disdain

But that's better anyway
It's just forgotten with the day
And it isn't alive
So it can't thrive

But you know,
Every sorrow
Does go away
Sometime, someday

Maybe, it's not time yet
Maybe, it's not the situation yet
For you to let go of it
But it will be, once you've learnt from it

There's a lot to learn
And a lot of yearn
And it's okay to take time
For it's your life, your time

9

I know you mean a lot to me
For I've been second guessing me
Do I really want what I do
Or do I just want some time and love from you?

Would I be willing to give it up for you?
Is a question that haunts me every day anew
I don't know the answer
Because I don't know your answer

The answer to the question I never asked
The answer to the question you never asked
We're both stuck, with silences in between
Waiting for the other person to begin the scene

I know there's something you wish to say
You know there's something I wish to say
But you wouldn't say it, and nor would I
And years down the line, we'd think of it and cry

Maybe we wouldn't, let's hope
Maybe these silences, we'd somehow cope
Someday, maybe we'd open up to each other
And say clearly what we wanted from the other

But these are maybes, and so are those
And I'd be a liar if I said I wasn't waiting for your rose
Maybe something sweet, or funny
Just something that reminds me of you, bunny

Maybe you're waiting, too
For me to come to you
And say what you want me to
But you know life won't let me do

Not that I wouldn't want to say it ever
Maybe that's what I've wanted forever
But you know, I'm a little old school
I believe in the love from before the cool

In handwritten letters and stolen glances
In smiling together despite circumstances
In the guy making the first move
That's what I want you to prove

That you're worth giving up everything for
That you're worth giving up my dreams for
Because once I'm yours, you'd be my dream come true
And you need to make me believe like that in you.

10
Just a moment or two
Spent with you
Makes my day
A happy day

You would probably never know
The feeling of the woe
Of not meeting you is for me
And how much it drains me of glee

You have no clue
How much I need you
Maybe not need, but look for
And how much I care for

Your actions have the capacity
To have the audacity
To hurt me so much more
Than could anyone else's lore

But I wouldn't tell you
For I don't want you
To know that you mean so much to me
For that'd only take you away from me

I know I can never be the girl you want
Never be the girl you can flaunt
Never be like her, who broke your heart
Yet, I know, somewhere, I do have a place in that heart

Maybe as a friend
Maybe a best friend
Maybe a confidant
Maybe an annoying debutante

But whatever it may be
It does give me glee
To be yours in my full capacity
And not want you to be mine in any capacity

11

Every day that I see you
And every day that I don't see you
Both mean so much to me
And both bring me glee

It's weird how that happens so much
It's funny how I feel so much
About you and me
And you away from me

I wonder if you see it that way
Because I don't know when is my last day
We might never see each other again
But maybe meet every time it does rain

I don't know if I'm being clear
But all I want is to keep you near
My heart and not my physical self
For that would mean you having to hold back yourself

And I wouldn't want you to do so
For any glee or any sorrow
Maybe one day, we'll see each other again
And realize we lost so much that we could gain

Maybe see the pieces of you in me
Maybe see the days you bring me glee
Maybe see the days you smile because of me
Or the days when you blush because of me

Maybe then, you'd see
That Maybe we're meant to be
Like they keep saying again and again
Maybe "us" is the end to your pain

But I'll not push you into it
Because it's your wish to do or forgo it
And trust me, I won't mind
For love looks not with the eyes, but the mind

But I'll be waiting for all the days
Till we finally have to separate our ways
For that one beautiful day of all these days
When we do try to join our ways

Maybe I'll fail, maybe I'll not
But it's a battle that ought to be fought
To win would be a win for me
And to lose would a win for glee

Maybe that'd teach me
That I don't need you for glee
That I'm complete in me
That I could be much more me.

12

I don't know why I play with fire
I don't know why I do admire
The things that I know will bring me pain
And nothing more but lots of disdain

Maybe there's a spark in being no more
Maybe there's a wish to go to one's core
Maybe the hope that will fire will burn away
Everything that stands in my way

Even if that's my own self and smile
Even if it's that extra mile
That I go everyday to see you
Every day is a pain anew

Maybe the fear that you'll somehow know
And never speak to me again once you know
Or the pain that you'll never be mine
Even if I put all efforts in line

Because I know you're not looking for me
But the long lost, long gone "she"
I understand your love for her though
And I am willing to go with the flow

For I've known you'll never be mine
So there's no further light to shine
I'm just enjoying the flow of time
Maybe, one day, do that, if you have the time.

13
Just a smile or two
Coming from you
Makes me forget all my woe
And makes me want time to go slow

It feels like the love they talk about
The one that the movies flout
As if I've fallen in the love the first time again
As if I've never known the heartbreak pain

And yet at night, it comes back
A reminder of everything I lack
To be the one you'd be in love with
Why I don't belong in that bandwidth

It haunts me till I fall asleep
It haunts me in my dreams so deep
The moments with you fill me with glee
And every moment after with a wish to flee

To go somewhere and do something
Something that would just bring
Me some peace and some love
The idea that I'd be the one you'd love

But that isn't possible anyway
For there is not a single day
When I wish for the same thing again
But end up with just more pain

But then, didn't I love you
Despite the faults in you?
But it'd be foolish of me
To expect the same from thee

Because you're not me
And you'd never understand me
But neither am I you
But at least I try to understand you

14

Some days it's a beautiful feeling
Some days just a pain reeling
Some days the hope
Some days the nope

Some days you're mine
Those days, my eyes shine
My smile's so true
As if I've been blessed anew

But there are days
When I realise that our ways
Will never be one
And you'll be, one day, just a no one

So will I be
And there's a pain in every glee
Every smile I have with you
With tears, I'll have to pay it back to you

For one day, you'll never look back
And I'll no more call you back
Because you never wanted to
And I got tired enough to

One day, maybe
You'll look back and see
Those smiles and wish for me
And maybe, even then, I'll be there for thee

Not as a significant other
But just a friend another
Maybe catch-up someday?
You'll text, and make me remember today.

15
It will never be me
It'll always be she over me
Despite what she did to you
And what I do for you

Because love is just a chance
Just fate's uncanny dance
Of who ends up loving whom
And who, in love, finds his doom

She'll always be your love
While I keep trying to earn a bit of that love
Or maybe, just care
But I know you won't care

Never did you do
Never will you do
Yet I keep my hopes high
Spread my wings as if I'll ever fly

Though I know I will never
She's your forever
And she'll always be
For in her, lies your glee

I can give up my life for you
But I'd still find you
Looking at her, or away
As if you'd never met me any day

I know you don't hate me at all
Just that you don't care at all
And so shouldn't I do
But I'm too attached to you

16
I wish I could
I surely would
But I somehow am unable to
Bring myself to

To get over you
To stay away from you
To stop falling for you
To somehow not love you

You seem like the reason
Why I was pushed into pain's season
Of why I needed to be here
When I so wanted to be there

Maybe I was sent because of you
But not sent for you
Maybe just to be there
Not for your love and care

I'll always want you
Or at least the good for you
Anyway, you'd never understand me
Because you never want to know me

17
I really want to
Somehow run into you
And meet you
Like we used to do

Carefree and smiling away
Looking forward to it the whole day
And smiling to our ears when we did meet
Never knowing the right way to greet

It was never a hi or a hello
As if you were my soul's fellow
Not just someone I'd met a month ago
But someone who'd seen me through my low

Sometimes your rawness scares me
Sometimes it brings me glee
For I know you don't show it to everyone
And it's nice to know I'm a close one

I don't know if you know
I miss that late night feeling of sorrow
And the talks we had about them all
Our lows, highs, rises and fall

Maybe we will, again, one day
And be weird again the next day
Because the depth can't be shown anymore
And the shallowness, we've crossed so much more

Maybe meet again one day
And we'll speak of the old day
The laughter and the tears
The joys and the fears

And I'll miss it again when you're gone
And think about you, forlorn
Pained in your pain and smiling in your glee
Sometimes, I think you're a best friend, truly

18

It feels so unreal
To be able to feel
So much and so deeply for you
Am I falling in love with you?

I wonder if I can ask you
Because you know love more than I do
You've loved before and you'll love again
For you believe in it despite the pain

It might not be me
Or it might be me
I don't care, it's not important to me
What matters is you are with me

The way you speak to me
The way you care for me
The way you smile when they talk about me
And the way you blush when they tease you about me

It makes me smile so much and so wide
As if in it, all my pains I could hide
And maybe some of your pains, too
But to share them with me is up to you

It's a nice feeling overall
Something I've never felt at all
Something I feel like I've wanted
And something that is just as sacred as haunted

Your smile, your words, your texts
Is all my heart expects
Every morning, afternoon and evening
As if you've finally given my life some meaning.

19

Every time I look at you
Every time I feel for you
It reminds of why I'm not the one
And why she was the one

You make me feel my lowest
When you're the one with whom time is slowest
You're the one whose actions make me feel alive
While your silences kill me alive

You are the one who I wish I'd never known
When you're the one who feels the farthest from unknown
You're the one I wish I'd never loved
When it's that love which makes me feel like I've finally lived

Why did we meet?
Why do you even greet?
Why do I even exist anymore
When the pain kills me to the core?

I don't have the answers, nor do you
All I know is that I really love you
And you don't, and you'll probably never do
While I'll be stuck with my feelings for you, maybe trying to get over you

20
Every morning
Is another mourning
And another life
Full of strife

I love you
I care for you
And you'll never love me
Or care for me

I try so hard each day
But you seem to have a way
To get back into my life
And bring more strife

Each time I think I'm over you
You make me realise I still love you
You still matter to me
Everything about you still affects me

Your smiles still bring me glee
I still love you more than me
You're still my first priority
Over my heart, you still have the authority

I still try to be like you
I still want to be loved by you
I still crave your presence
And I still die in your absence

Why don't you just go away?
Why don't you just leave my way?
If you're never meant to be mine
Why don't you just let me untwine?

21
Maybe you do love me
May you do care for me
Maybe my smiles do bring you glee
Maybe you do smile for me

But you're too shy to say
Maybe blushing is your way
To say what is unsaid
Maybe we share the same dread

Of not being enough for the other
Of losing them to some another
Who'd be better and more suited
Someone whose love is more undisputed

You hide behind your past
And I hide in my cast
I cry alone, saying you don't love me
And you'll never love me

But maybe you do
Or maybe it's my mind's updo
Maybe I'm so in love with you
That I can't fathom the idea of love without you

I'm scared of my love for you
What if you also do?
What if you come up and say?
What would the future way?

Will we be compatible enough?
Will I be able to love you enough?
Will we be able to make it through?
Will we be able to stay relevant and true?

What if we can't bear the weight of love?
What if we get into a mess, some kind of?
What if you stop loving me?
What if you start hating me?

But any of these isn't going to be true
For you'll never feel for me, would you?
I know you won't, you'll stay stuck with 'she'
Never even realizing anything about me

You'll probably never know I love you
And I don't even want you to
I'll lose you altogether then
And I don't want that, at least not so sudden

I've just met you
Just fallen for you
Let me at least learn to start moving on
Don't just get so withdrawn

Not so soon, not today
Maybe some other day
When I'm not so much in love with you
When I can actually walk away from you

22

Falling in love again
Even though I know it'll bring me pain
For nothing lasts forever as is
And probably I'll never be able to be his

Will he love me back, is a question that haunts me
But every time he speaks to me, it brings me pure glee
Maybe he will, one fine day, my heart does whisper
Maybe I am in love with you, I wish he'd whisper

I know I sound like a teenager in love
But that is the beauty of love
Nothing remains but itself
Nothing matters but itself

Maybe we'd go on a date to your favourite bar
And you'd drive us there, in your car
And we'd come back early, to complete your project
And spend the rest of the night writing that project

Wake up the next morning with a bundle of pages
And your dreamy, half asleep eyes would remind me of sages
And the magic they say they had
I'd seen all of it in your eyes, my dear lad

Maybe ruffle your hair and wake you up
After writing the pages when you were asleep and I was up
Fix your smile and see you off
And then remembering I had to see myself off

Maybe I'm dreaming as I always do
But my dreams could be brought to life by you
For you're my dream come true
Don't know why, but I do love you

23

Do you remember the day I met you
The day I first saw you
Because I do
And I hope you do, too

That day in college, maybe
When you hadn't probably seen me
Or noticed me, for that matter
Even I hadn't noticed much, for the same matter

But remember when we met the first time?
We clicked like we'd been friends for the longest time
I'd never spoken so much to a stranger ever
And I don't think I'd do that again in forever

But it seemed so natural with you
As if I'd always known you
Maybe it wasn't that special for you
Making a friend anew

But it was so special for me
And you became special for me
With time, I fell for you
And so did you

And it's been the best journey since
Never did you let pain make me wince
Always by my side, always there for me
I don't know if I've been there that much for thee

But all I was to say is thank you
And that I really love you
Thank you for being with me and bearing with me
And being the reason for my never ending glee

24
I try so hard every day
To find fault in my way
Of where I fall short
And where she didn't fall short

I compare myself every night to her
Go to bed thinking of her
Because you still love her, despite everything
And you'll never love me, despite everything

Every morning, I wake up with a pain
And every night, I sleep with disdain
You'll never love me, you'll never be mine
And your presence will never let me untwine

I'm so done with myself
So done with what I have of myself
So done with how I look and how I am
Seems like my entire existence is a sham

Even I want to be loved, is that too much to ask?
Is loving me such a huge task?
That no one's ever wanted to do
And neither will you

And why would you?
When you've got a long line of girls for you
Waiting for you, whom you could possibly love
And not me, with someone you'd never associate love

I wish I was her, or she was me
At least I'd know that the fault wasn't in me
That I wasn't not enough
And since I do, life is rough

I wish you'd love me
Or get away from me
So that I could forget you
Forget that I ever loved you

Because I'm tired of being me
And the realization that you'll never love me
There's little I can do about the first one
Each day leaves me feeling more undone

I'm tired of trying so hard
It's only making life hard
Because there seems to be no improvement
There seems to be no development

I don't want to lose myself to you
And not even find you
I just want to go back to when I didn't know you
To when I didn't love you

To when I was more me than you
To when I hadn't lost so much of myself to you
To when I was still me
To when I was smiling in genuine glee

25

I don't know why
Some night I do cry
In my heart
As if it's still broken into part

You left so long back
And I repaired myself back
Forgave that you gave me so much pain
Learnt to get over that disdain

Of having wasted so much of my life on you
On having even loved you
On having literally worshipped you
On being the one to always forgive you

Forgave myself for praying for you
For always being there for you
For always trying to be good enough for you
When I was always better than you

Yet when I saw you today
My heartbeat did fade away
I still felt a shock in my chest
As if my heart had been laid to rest

I saw that picture again
And I felt so much pain
So much that it felt I had died
But alas, I hadn't even cried

But I did go back to normal soon
As if it was just that the clouds had hidden the moon
Maybe I'll get better at not hurting for you
As I move farther away from you

But I've moved so far away
That I don't think of you ever, any day
Maybe there's a longer way to go
And trust me, I'm willing to go

I'd loved you
I don't hate you
And I don't think that's wrong
Because to forgive is a sign of the strong

And I've forgiven myself and you, too
For all that you've made me go through
For I've loved and not wanted anything
And I know now it was never a mutual feeling

Goodbye to you
Goodbye to my pain from you
Goodbye to the girl who loved you
And goodbye to the girl who was affected by you

26

The girl you see
The one who seems to be brimming with glee
Smiling and laughing around
Have you ever heard her mind's sound?

Have you ever asked her if she's okay?
If she's able to go through her day?
If she's able to sleep at night?
If she's gripped by some fright?

You never did and you never will do
For she seems alright to you
And so does she want to
Because she wants to hide it from you

Because she doesn't want you to know
That she's feeling so low
And it's all because of you
Because she is so in love with you

And she feels you'll never love her back
Because there's something that she does lack
That she's not pretty enough for you
That she's not interesting enough for you

That you'll never look at her that way
That you'll never be hers any day
That you'll never love her ever
And that she'll never have her forever

Because she saw it all with you
She dreamt her fairy-tale with you
You're her dream come true
And yet, she'll never have you

Maybe she'll heal on her own
Maybe she'll have grown
By the time you realise it
She'll probably have grown over it

She's a strong girl after all
She knows how to get up after a fall
You might be her dream come true
But she's got much more in life than just you

27

Just remembered the old days
Days before we parted ways
Never did it become clear
But it was never unclear

We were probably never meant to be
And I'm glad you saw that before me
I'd have hurt myself a lot before I saw so
But you saved me from a lot of sorrow

Not that I look back and see
I see a beauty in me
And a grace and elegance in you
For not letting me get hurt for you

Thank you for coming into my life
And for walking away without causing strife
You knew you could stay
And I'd never push you away

But you saw that would hurt me somewhere
And maybe that was your form of care
To let me heal from wounds that could've been
Had you not walked away after you'd seen

Maybe you know me more than me
And you do care about my glee
And it's okay to walk away at times
Things are just not meant to be, at times

Sometimes I wish they'd been
What a beautiful future that'd have been
But anyway, that doesn't matter anymore
All I have to say is thank you, from my core

28

I wish you were in love with me
The way I am in love with thee
We'd stay up till late
Smiling as your gaze accelerates my heart rate

We'd go to the terrace
Maybe simply race
And I'd lose it to you
Because I love winning on you

We'd stay there and chat about our days
About what all we did and our ways
Discuss the small and big things
And the emotions that it brings

We'd speak of the old days
When we would cross ways
And never even met each other
Though we were so near each other

And now that we're not
See how close we've been brought
By love and love only
Being far yet never feeling lonely

Maybe I'd see that day
Maybe we'd live to see that day
When we're together
So in love with each other

29

I'm tired of this
I don't want any more of this
I'm tired of loving you
And not being loved by you

Not being loved is still fine
But what do you have against all that's mine?
Why do you ignore me so much?
Why do you hate me so much?

What have I done to you
That has ever hurt you?
I've said sorry even when I wasn't wrong
And forgiven you without a sorry for your wrong

Given you chances again and again
And all you've given me is pain
I'm tired of not being able to get over you
Tired of being so much in love with you

I wish I could help you
But you wouldn't let me do
I wish you would speak to me
I'm tired of being ignored by thee

You knew of my health deteriorating
Yet you kept me waiting
You were sitting right next to me
Yet you didn't speak to me

You didn't even look at me
You could've simply asked me
If I was fine or not, just like you do
Each time one of them is ill and they tell you

I wonder if you care about me at all
If you think of my existence at all
If you care if I'm even dead or alive
When, to be perfect for you, I strive

Every story of mine begins with you
And so does each one end on you
You are mean so much to me
Do I mean nothing at all to thee?

30

To speak to me, you don't have the time
But you keep speaking to her all the time
Sometimes I feel like hating myself
For loving you with all of myself

And maybe I've started hating myself again
Because of your pain
Because I know you'll never love me
No matter what, I'll never be good enough for thee

And I hate myself for not being able to
Simply walk away and get over you
Just like you've always done and still do
It's just so simple for you

One girl to the next
And from that one to the next
And again and again and again
And each time, it gives me pain

For never being even one of them for you
For not being able to enchant you
For not being able to simply be yours
My heart feels dry and throat coarse

I wish I could tell you
How much I do love you
But for that, you'd need to speak to me
Which, it seems like, is too much to ask of thee

I know I will never have you
Yet my heart yearns for you
Yet my first thought each morning is you
And everything somehow reminds me of you

I wish it was just so simple for me
To walk away and get over thee
I would surely do that for me
And more than me, probably for thee

For you seem to want to get rid of me
And I can't seem to walk away from thee
It would've been so simple if I could just
Maybe life would've been simpler to adjust

31

You spoke not to her, but me
Initially it did bring me glee
That you chose me
But then I realised it was just a game for thee

Speak to one and not the other
Ignore one for another
Playing with us as toys
Choosing us for instant joys

Whoever seemed easier to speak to
Whoever would be more fun to you
As if we weren't women
But just toys for you men

Thankfully we didn't lose the friendship
While looking for your relationship
Which neither of us ever got
But, over you, we never even fought

She's my best friend till date
And she's helped me so much of late
Which I'm sure you'd never do
For you'd always be too busy with you

I'm glad we got over you
And none of us got into a relationship with you
It'd have broken both of us
And also the bond between us

32

I'm tired of being there for you
Of being so much in love with you
When I know you'll never be there for me
Or feel anything for me

I'm just another passer-by in your life
But you occupy such a huge part of my life
So much that it seems dull without you
So much that it feels mundane without you

I'm tired of being the only one in love
Tired of giving away all the love
And yet I don't know why
I can't get over you, no matter how hard I try

I know you'll never be mine
I know you'll never even think of being mine
And yet I think of being yours all day
For you keep popping up in my head in some or the other way

I don't know why I even love you
There's nothing so special about you
And yet I'm in love with all you lack
Instead of just walking back

Back to where I've been for so long
Back to where I feel strong
Back to when I was far from you
And so very far from being in love with you

33

I don't know why
My heart still does cry
It still pins for you
Even though it knows you

It knows that you'll never look at me
And feel the innocent glee
That I feel by looking at you
For I am in love with you

It knows you'll never be
Just as deeply in love with me
For I'm not the kind
Who could just blow your mind

I'm the kind who you can run back to
Not the one who'd enchant the wits out of you
The one you could cry your pains to
Not the one who's smile would bewitch you

And that's probably why
My mind still does cry
Of why I can't get over you
When I don't mean anything like that to you

Honestly speaking, I know you
More than even you do
I know it sounds like a lie
But you can ask and try

I've noticed so much
Because I've loved so much
And so deeply
That every breath of yours I've seen keenly

As if you were the best work of art
As if you were life's most important part
As if I knew you were my reason to be
Just because your presence brought me glee

But it never was, and it will never be
And it's okay if it'll never be me
I don't even ask for that anymore
All I want is to be smiling to the core

Both you and me
Each basking in our own glee
Smiling and laughing away
For real, maybe, one day

For I see the tears you don't shed away
The fears that haunt you each day
The memories that hurt you
Each time when silence surrounds you

I hope you can smile one day
In a true and honest way
A smile that'd be from your heart's core
That all I want, nothing more.

34

There might still be a pain
But there's no more disdain
It doesn't hurt so much anymore
Not all the way to the core

I know I did love you
And you know what you did do
But I don't love you anymore
Not do I have the time to hate you anymore

I'm done wasting my time on you
On feeling so much for you
On loving you so much that I forgot myself
But you never got enough time from yourself

I know you'll yell at me
If I ever tell any of these to thee
But I'm absolutely done with you
I no longer have anything to do with you

I can't say nothing about your matters anymore
But one day, it won't matter anymore
I'm sure I'll take myself to that day
Somehow, through some way

I knew back then, too
That you didn't love me, too
But I didn't know this about you
That you hated me because I loved you

Sometimes I wish I did know
But it'd only have increased my woe
Anyway, I'm thankful I didn't
And you never made a hint

You could've simply walked up to me
And said you didn't love me
I wouldn't have hurt you for that
Just as you shouldn't have hurt me for that

But you are you and I am me
And so will I always be
I never did and I never will
Pray for anything but for your goodwill

May you be happy wherever you are
May you keep shining like a star
Stay away from me, if you will
Because I don't hate you and I never will

35
If I ever fall in love with you
I'll make sure you know it, too
But I'll never say it to you
Because I don't know how to

And I don't think I ever will learn to
For I'll be so busy loving you
That I'll not ever realize
When I forget to have my tries

At learning how to say it
I'll even forget I don't know it
Because love will be
All that'll be in me

All that is in my mind
Currently, is to be kind
So kind that never can you
Complain about what I didn't do

And yet, I know
There'll be some people who'll call me shallow
Just because I want to be
Kind to a point of glee

But I won't care
About their snare
Because I'll be too busy with
What I've found my happiness with

And let me tell you
That I mean to thank you
For always standing by my side
For being someone in whom I can confide

Thank you for coming into my life
And helping me get on with life
When I thought I was nothing anymore
Thank you for showing my sorrow the way to the door

Thank you for making me
Smile and learn to feel the glee
That was always within me
Which I couldn't see

36

I will never say that I love you
For I don't know how to
And I'll never learn to
For I'll be busy in loving you

But I'll leave hints here and there
Show you that I do care
About everything related to you
And that I feel something for you

I may Show it to you
But I won't say it to you
And it'll be up to you
If you can add up the clue

But I'll be a fun game either way
Whether you do find a way
Or not, to the truth waiting for you
To the truth that says I love you

I'll wait for as long as you play
For you'll be my world that day
And for as long as you want to
For my love for you is really true

37

I loved you more than I loved me
That's where it started to be
The pain that I feel today
And the disdain that I healed yesterday

If only I'd loved you
Just as I should've loved you
As an equal, as a mate
I probably wouldn't have suffered your hate

You disliked me
Because I worshipped thee
I gave you the place
Of my solace

I gave you the position of my God
But you didn't know how to be God
And hence, you mistreated me
And that's a curse that stays with me

A curse from a God who didn't know
There was a protocol for Gods to follow
That they were to love and bless
And not just make other people's lives a mess

But I don't blame you
Because you didn't know what to do
And I didn't know that you didn't know
And probably that's why the sorrow

Someone told me about you today
That you're happy and successful in your own way
And that didn't make me feel anything
Except for the void where used to lie my everything

My universe revolved around you
I lived my life for you
I spent my nights praying for you
And my days hoping to somehow have a glimpse of you

I loved you as I've never heard of
And I hope to never hear of
Because no one deserves to be through
Even half of what you made me go through

You misused my love against me
You made sure you made me hate me
To the extent that I feared
Each time a mirror neared

I was scared of every part of me
Because you made me
You made me feel like I was ugly
When it was you who couldn't be me

You were intimidated of me
And of what was my potential to be
And yet I never saw any of it
I was too busy loving you to notice any of it

And you destroyed me part by part
Broke down my entirety part by part
I wonder how someone could be
The stone hearted person you were to me

I wonder how you could be
The person who hated me
Just for being in love with you
Just for praying for you

But you are you, and so will you be

And I will always be me
I won't hate you and you won't love me
But one thing has changed, I don't love thee

Not anymore, not any longer
You made my resolve to leave stronger
I tried my best to stay
And you made sure I had to go away

You hated me so much
That my love couldn't stand such
So much negativity you poured into me
That I had no choice but to go away from thee

And now that I'm so far away
I realize I took the right way
Because I finally chose me
Finally learnt to be me

Finally learnt that there was a me
A person who also deserved glee
A person beyond thee
A person with a lot of potential to be

I won't hate you ever
But never will I be able to love you ever
Hate me or not, just stay away from me
For I don't want to bring back the memories of thee

I don't want to suffer the pain
Of what you did, again and again
I don't love you anymore
But sometimes it does hurt to the core

But I'll surely heal again
From all the hurt and the pain

And I promise you
I'll build myself up anew

I'll not be
The girl I used to be
The girl who loved you
The girl who was hated by you

I'll be the woman who
Will not be affected by you
Will not be hurt again
And will have healed from the pain

38

I wish I could go back
And tell myself long back
That I needed to go
And not keep feeling so low

And yet so full of hope
For the answer would always be a nope
You'd never love me
And never care for the love you got from me

You'd never care for me
Or about the fact that I lived for thee
Whenever I did pray
It was always for you, no matter when, which day

It was always for you, never for me
I don't even remember a time when I didn't pray for thee
When I was still me
And not just a shadow for thee

Just another woman, I would end up to be
For you never valued me
You never saw anything
For you, I was never anything

And yet, for me
My world revolved around thee
Everything that I was and I would be
I wanted to share it with thee

I would get up everyday
Just so that I could pray
For your exams to go well
Even on days when I was unwell

Even when I needed to rest
My heart was at unrest
Because I was worried about you
Worried about how you'd do

And trust me
I've never seen anyone but me
Pray so much and with so much love
That they forgot about getting any love

I never even saw what you did do
That you hated me for loving you
For being the one who
Would never leave you

Who would've stayed at all times
No matter how hard her own times
Who would've been with you
Even when you hated her through and through

But you couldn't see
The purity in me
The divinity in my love for you
The truth in my prayers for you

You kept hating me
And I kept loving thee
Till time pushed me away
From the hate that was eating me away

When I had to go
Because time made me go
Because you pushed me so far
That I had no choice but to be afar

And with solace and time, did I learn to

Start unloving you
And love myself
To live for my own self

And it's been so long to that day
I've changed in my own way
And yet one thing remains in me
I could never hate you for hating me

I'm still the one who does love
But this time, it's the whole world I love
Not just you, never again you
While I know you still hate me, don't you?

I've forgiven you
What else was there to do?
And I don't even care
The past is no more a scare

I live on
I love on
And so will I continue to
Till my last breath, always and anew

Loving you might did lead me
To where I was supposed to be
Away from you, but not away
From the fact that loving was my way

I did fall in love again
And it didn't bring me pain
It's a beautiful feeling
And it helps my healing

He's nothing like you
And so is nothing that he does do

There are scars and they will be
Till time let's me heal all the pain I've gotten from thee

They tell me you're in a happy place
And I hope you've found the right place
For I wish no harm to you
I never did and would never do

39

Each day the pain consumes me
And yet it never bothers thee
I wonder how you could be
So heartless about what you did to me

You broke my heart
Into a million part
And not simply, in just a day
But in the worst way

You broke me piece by piece
Stole my soul's peace
Made me hate myself
All because I loved you more than myself

Because I forgot to
Draw a line for you
A line that separated me
From all the pains that you gave me

A line you were not supposed to cross
A boundary you were not to step across
A way to protect myself from you
From the hate I got from you

The hate I mistook for love
That I got in return for my love
Because I didn't know thee
And you didn't understand me

You still don't
And I know you won't
Because you don't want to
And now, I don't even want you to

I'm done with you
With everything to do with you
With everything that I gave you
And everything that I got from you

This is the final goodbye
This time, I won't even cry
Because this is a decision I take for me
For my soul, for my glee

40

I wish I could undo
What all I did in my love for you
Though I wouldn't undo
All I did for you

Because I did it out of love
And nothing but just pure love
But I'd still undo all that I did to me
When I was in love with thee

I'd undo all the pain
That I went through again and again
Only because of you
Only because you didn't love me as I loved you

And I still thought that there was something in you
Something that was humane in you
Something that would probably love me
At least love my love for thee

But you weren't that bare minimum
And my love for you was at its maximum
It had always been that way
And so would it stay till the very last day

You didn't deserve anything
Yet I gave you everything
And what did you give me?
You hated me for loving thee

At every step, every single time
You humiliated me each time
Never did you leave me
Smiling with glee

And never did I
Not come home and cry
But even then, each day
It was for you that I did pray

I loved you more than can be
And you still hated me
Probably they're right when they say
That not everyone deserves to be loved that way

They probably say it about you
About the fact that nothing could ever change you
That no matter how much I loved you
You hated me through and through

Even stones turn soft when prayed to
But even that didn't happen with you
I wonder how you could do
All you made me go through

41

Each time the question arose
It was you I chose
Over my own self, over me
Over my happiness, my glee

I prayed for you
Even when I needed it, too
I loved you
Even when hate was all I got from you

I was ignored, humiliated, and so much more
Broken down to the core
And yet with all my pieces, I loved you
More than I knew I could do

I loved you like I've never heard of
A story I hope to never hear of
I don't want anyone else to go through
Anything of what you made me go through

You broke me
While I prayed for thee
You humiliated me
While I loved thee

I wish somehow you understood me
Understood my love for thee
Understood that I loved you
And not anything that was associated with you

I loved you to a fault
And that was my fault
To put you over me
Over my ambitions and glee

I was ready to give up everything for you
Give up my existence for you
But you didn't ask for my life
You made me go through hell during life

You didn't tell me
That you hated me
You showed it to me
How much you hated me

And why did you hate me?
For the fact that I loved thee?
That I cared for you
That I lived for you

You were my everything
And I knew that for you, I was nothing
Yet I loved you each day
In every possible way

But you never understood the value of that love
You poisoned that love
So much that it got toxic for me
Even then, I loved thee

I loved you despite everything
Despite my own suffering
And what did you do?
Hated me more each day, didn't you?

I hope that one day
You learn about love in some way
You learn that love isn't easy to do
And especially when the other person doesn't love you

I did all I could

More than you ever would
But I failed, I failed miserably
And I went back terribly

It broke me
To no more love thee
But I learnt each day
A new survival way

And slowly I began to live again
To live despite the pain
To cry at night and heal the next morning
To live in a constant mourning

And it took me
Years to rebuild me
From what you made me go through
All for being in love with you

I don't want to say anything to you
There's nothing to say to you
You know what you did
Each of them was a well planned deed

But anyway, I won't wish you ill
I never did and I never will
May you be happy wherever you are
But just a single request, remain afar

I'm tired of crying
While I'm trying
To be
That which is not me

Tired of trying to be
Good enough for thee
In the process, losing me
And not even having thee

Honestly speaking, I'd do
All of this for you
All over again
Without thinking of the pain

For I'm ready to lose me
Just to have thee
To be able to be loved by you
I'm ready to be who you want me to

But it doesn't seem so
There seems no end to this sorrow
I lose myself for you
And yet it doesn't affect you

You still don't look at me
The way I look at thee
You don't love me
No matter how much I love thee

I wish I could say it to you
That I love you
But I don't know how to
Say it to you

And I probably never will be able to
Learn how to say it to you
Because I am scared to say it to you
And, in doing so, lose you

Lose you what I have of you
As what you let me have of you
Even though you ignore me
I still love thee

And I don't know why I do
Still fall in love with you
Each day, each time
More than the previous time

Even though you don't even look at me
My eyes never lose sight of thee
I could tell you in the midst of a crowd
Recognize your voice in the middle of music so loud

But you don't even care
That I'm always there
That I keep showing you
That I do love you

I wish it wasn't so
I wouldn't be drowning in sorrow
And in love at the same time
Each day, all the time

But this is what is to be
What I get for loving thee
When you don't love me
When you don't care about me

43

When I look at pictures of you
I don't feel anything for you
I wonder if I've actually fallen out of love with you
Or if this is just another trap laid by you

If there's something you still want out of me
If there's still a desire to break me
Into pieces so small that I can't even pick them up
And so sharp that they hit me each time I get up

If you wanted me to
I'd simply die for you
But you didn't want that to be
You wanted to hurt me

To break me in a million ways
Through a gazillion number of days
So that I could never be
What used to be of me

And yet I loved you
More than you could ever do
To anyone or anything
You didn't even understand that feeling

And it was wrong of me
To love thee
It was not the love that was wrong
It was simply too strong

Too strong to see
What you were doing to me
How you were breaking me
Killing away all my glee

But it never did see
For it never saw anyone but thee
And I saw with love's eyes
Which saw everything but lies

And all you did was to lie
Which is probably why I still do cry
For all I lost was love
Simple and pure love

That's probably why it hurt me
And nothing happened to thee
When I did walk away
Because you just lost a human, but I lost love that day

44

I used to wonder how it would be
To fall out of love with thee
I could imagine my life without you
And now, I don't even think of you

Not on most days
Sometimes, never, for a stretch of days
It's almost like you never came into my life
And filled it up to the brim with strife

But I don't blame you
Because my love was too strong for you
For you to able to
Understand what I felt for you

It was too strong for you
To be able to love me, too
Because no matter how much you'd love me
My love was always stronger than thee

So you decided not to love me
But to break me
Into the smallest possible pieces
Into intangible pieces

Pieces that couldn't be joined again
Pieces that'd always bring me pain
That'd always remind me
Of my unending love for thee

Which was forced to end
Which was poisoned till the very end
So much that it almost killed me
In the effort of loving thee

But I still did so
No matter how much the sorrow
No much how much you hurt me
Because I never saw anything but your glee

I couldn't see it at all
How you were bringing my downfall
How you were breaking me down
How you were trying to steal my crown

But you failed in doing so
Yes, you did bring me sorrow
And you did break me
But my love made a Phoenix out of me

I rose from my ashes yet again
Stronger than ever before, from the pain
I don't hate you at all
For bringing my downfall

Because you only made me stronger
Made my love all the more stronger
Which now is for the entire world
Considering you were once my entire world

For that was what used to be
You meant the entire universe to me
But now the entire universe is mine to love
Which, now, I am strong enough to love

45
I forgive you
For all that you made me go through
But can you,
Forgive yourself for all that you did do?

Can you forgive yourself for each time that you did try
To break me down to the point that I did cry?
Can you forgive yourself for all the times you hated me
And made me suffer, only because I loved thee?

Can you forgive yourself for all my tears?
For being the reason love is one of my fears?
For giving me so much pain?
For filling my heart with disdain?

Can you forgive yourself for all my sleepless nights I spent crying?
Only because you hated me for trying
For trying to be good enough for you
Even when I was already better than you

Can you forgive yourself for all the days you ignored me
Made me feel so underneath thee?
Can you?
I know it's not easy to

And I don't know what to say
Except that I didn't deserve to be hurt that way
Yet I forgave you
And to this day, I do

I don't hold a grudge against you
For I had loved you
Love so simple and pure
In which lied every ailment's cure

And so did lie the cure to my pain
The key to healing my disdain
The strength to forgive you
Despite all that you made me go through

I hope you can do the same, too
Forgive yourself for what you made me go through
Because you were the one who actually lost
I lost a person, but it was true love that you lost

And I really am sorry for your loss
It's an irreplaceable loss
Because love like that exists only in books now
Or in love stories that fate doesn't allow

But you lost it all
When you had it all
And I feel bad for you
Now that I have healed from all that you made me go through

46
I wish I could be
The one loved by thee
The one you wanted
And not the most unwanted

And it's not like I didn't try
Not like my heart didn't cry
While leaving all of me
To be the one for thee

But even then, you didn't want me
Even when it was all according to thee
All according to how you wanted it to be
And yet, you didn't love me

I tried so very hard
Worked so hard
And yet, I failed
My love failed

I loved you
Despite the imperfections in you
Despite the faults in you
Despite the issues I had to deal with, because of you

But you didn't love me
Even when I lost myself for thee
Lost everything I was to be
Everything that was loved by thee

I lost everything
And earned nothing
But the most important thing was
I lost it all for a Cause

I lost it for love
I lost it to love
And I was true
In my love for you

And so, it's not wrong to
Try to do things for you
To leave it all for you
Or to be something just to be loved by you

I had already left my dreams for you
Because you seemed to be my dream come true
But you weren't so
And that filled me with sorrow

I wish you'd seen me
Seen everything I did for thee
Noticed how I changed myself
To suit yourself

But didn't see it
You simply couldn't see it
For you never saw me
And my eyes never left thee

But I don't blame you
I don't blame myself, too
It was just as it was supposed to be
I was to learn to never lose myself for someone else's glee

47

I wish I was what you wanted
Who you wanted
Who you loved the way
I love you, even today

But you didn't see
Anything to love in me
Anything to care about
Didn't see a woman you could flout

Show off as your girlfriend
Or even a casual friend
Because I wasn't showy
I'm still not showy

You couldn't see
The depth within me
For you didn't want to see
Anything but the superficiality in me

And I'm anything but superficial
I can't even be superficial
Not even for you
Not even for my love for you

I wish I'd seen
What you'd been
And understood
The lies under your hood

The lies you kept telling me
The lies you kept showing me
The lies you kept proving to me
Till I found out you didn't love me

And trust me
That hurt me
It broke me
Made it impossible to say anything to thee

Because you didn't tell me
You didn't break me
But I was broken because of you
Because of my love for you

And even to this day
I can't think of the way
The way of lies you walked me through
The way you treated me all through

Did you never think of me?
Of my love for thee?
Of all the lies you told me
What if I caught thee?

What would be of me
If I came to know the truth of thee
You didn't think that it'd shatter me?
Make life so painful that there'd never be a place for glee?

Did you ever do that?
Even think of doing that?
You didn't, and will never do
Because you can't see anything over you

You can't see
What you made of me
How you broke me
How you almost killed me

And yet I didn't die
I couldn't even cry
What would I cry for?
What was there to cry for?

You didn't love me
You never felt for me
It was as simple as that
And would always be that

I wish there was a way
To change that day
The day I fell in love with you
And each day, that I loved you

But there isn't a way
To go back to that day
And tell myself to
Not fall for you

You've broken me
Sucked away all my glee
I wish you'd at least see
What you did to me

But you don't
And I know you won't
Not even if I cry
Not even if I die

48

I would be
What you wanted me to be
If you ever loved me
I'd have given up myself for thee

But you didn't care
You look here and there
And never at me
Never ever at me

You didn't bother to see
The pain in me
The fact that you were hurting me
By going on playing with me

I was as human as you
And much more humane than you
But, back then, I could never see
Any fault in thee

You were always right
Never realized you were the cause of my plight
The reason I cried myself to sleep each night
The reason why my mornings weren't bright

You reminded me
Each time that you saw me
That you didn't love me
That I wasn't deserving of thee

That couldn't care less of me
Or of anything about me
That it didn't matter to you
If I existed or didn't do

And probably
You'd be better off without me
And that it's be better if I wasn't there
Or anywhere

That you hated me
For being me
For living life
The way I lived life

You hated me
For loving thee
For caring for you
For never giving up on you?

I wanted to ask
But it was too much of a task
Because as much as I loved you
I was scared of you

Scared of what you'd say
If I spoke to you someday
If I asked you something
What if you broke my everything?

So I never said a word to you
Never asked anything to you
But never did I
Ever make you cry

And I couldn't do so
Even today, I can't do so
Because I'm not heartless like you
And I still don't hate you

Even after all that you made me go through

After all the insults I got from you
All the pain
All the disdain

No, I don't hate you
And will never do
Because I'm not you
And can never be you

49
You're always on my face
Be it in pain or in solace
Be it when I want to die
Or when I just want to cry

You've given me
In return for your glee
A mountain of pain
And an ocean of disdain

And I took it from you
Because I loved you
And anything from thee
Meant more than anything to me

Even the pain
Even disdain
Felt like a gift
My favourite gift

Each tear
Each fear
Because of you
Felt like a gift anew

Each time I cried
A part of me died
The girl in me screamed
The devil in you beamed

Each time I was too scared to
Even speak to you
My inside hurt so much
And your insides smiled so much

And I smiled, too
Because I saw a smile on you
Because I saw you happy
It made me happy

I loved you
More than I could do
More than I've ever seen
More than it should've been

And even today
I don't regret a single day
That I spent loving you
Because I learnt a lot from you

You didn't teach me
But I learnt from thee
I learnt how to strive
How to survive

How to be happy
When there's no glee
How to smile everyday
When life breaks you in every way

You taught me
What no one could've taught me
What no one would be able to
Because I never loved anyone as I loved you

And that's why
Even though I do cry
I don't hate you
Don't hold anything against you

Because what you taught me
Means more to me
Than all the pain you gave me
You made me a better version of me

And I thank you
For cutting me through
For breaking me
For shattering me

I'd have never learnt how to
Survive without you
Had it not been for you
For how much I was hurt by you

I'd have never learnt to be
What is, today, of me
Without you
And, for that, I thank you

50
All my love and care
Was your worst nightmare
For you didn't know how to
Deal with my love for you

You had never been
Covered by love's sheen
Never been seen the way
I saw you back in the day

Never knew what it was to be
The centre of the universe for me
Didn't know what to do
Each time I met you

Even I didn't know
That you didn't know
Even if I knew
There was little I could do for you

Love wasn't a choice for me
It was a way of living to me
I lived through love
And was shattered by love

Maybe I don't
And I won't
Love you again
Because of the pain

But now I understand you
Understand your view
Yet, I can't justify
The way you made me cry

The way you broke me
Hurt me
Made me feel so low
Caused me so much woe

Made me feel unloved
When all I did was loved
And loved so much and so true
Loved no one but you

I might be biased here
But it's because I did care
More than I've seen anyone do
More than I could do

But I'm not here
To tell you I did care
Because you do know it
More than I knew it

I just wanted to say
I forgive you for each day
That you broke me
That you hurt me

That you misunderstood me
That you ended my glee
For each day
When you looked away

When you ignored me
When you insulted me
Humiliated me
Degraded me

I forgive you

But it's not because I love you
I did love you
But I no longer feel for you

And I promise to
Never again feel for you
I might've forgiven you
But there's no way I could forget you

Forget everything
That reduced me to nothing
That almost killed me
And left me to be

51
Each time I care
I'm met with despair
Each time I love
I'm met with everything but love

But each time
Is just another time
With you
For you

About you
To you
Near you
What if it's not love, but you?

The fact that you
Don't love me, too
The fact that you
Don't care, too

The reality that you don't want me
And I want nothing but thee
Is that what is hurting me
Or is there more to the story?

I wish there was more
More to endure
But it doesn't seem to be
Anything but endless pain for me

For you, a person to ignore
And not care for anymore
A person to hate again
To give more pain

I don't know why
You can't see me cry
Even when I do
Even when I'm crying right in front of you

Even when you do know
Why my tears flow
Why do you not do something
Instead of avoiding me and my feeling?

Why do you?
Why don't you?
I want to ask you
But I won't do

Because I don't know
If you'll cause me more woe
Or set me free
From the pain within me

And I'm not willing to
Take the risk with you
My experience tells me not to
And your eyes force me not to

52

You broke me into pieces
And I loved you with all the pieces
I loved you to the point of disdain
And you filled my life with pain

I tried my best to
Keep loving you
And you did your best to
Make sure I wasn't able to

I don't know why
You did try
To make me
Unlove thee

I don't understand why
You made me cry
When all I was trying to do
Was to help you

To help you be
What you needed to be
What you deserved to be
What was your potential to be

I don't know how
You broke me somehow
And broke me so
That you filled each breath with sorrow

You killed me
But death didn't come to be
I couldn't do away
I had to suffer each day

I had to be
The one without the glee
The one filled with pain
The one dealing with disdain

I was to be
What I didn't deserve to be
Just because I loved you
And believed in you

Because I saw in you
What no one else could do
Because I saw that you could do
All that you wanted to

That you were capable enough to
Make all your dreams come true
That you deserved to be
All you dreamt to be

Was that wrong of me
To believe in thee?
To believe that you could do
All you wanted to?

To admire you?
To understand you?
To pray for you?
To love you?

I don't think so
And never will I think so
You could kill my love for you
But you could never make me you

I still carry love with me
No matter where I be
I still believe in it
Even if mine didn't requite

53

I wish you loved me
As I loved thee
I wish you cared, too
Just as I had dared to

It wasn't as tough for thee
As it was for me
It wasn't as scary for you
As painful as it was me to go through

It wouldn't have been so
There wouldn't have been so much sorrow
Had you been able to
See what I felt for you

To be able to
Understand my feelings for you
Understand how I felt
Maybe you'd have known how I was to be dealt

I understand you didn't love me
I always knew this within me
And I never loved you
With the expectation of being loved by you

I knew it was never to be
That you would ever love me
And I didn't need thee
To say the same to me

But what did you do?
Made me dream of you
Made me believe that you loved me
Made me dream of a future with thee

And in small hits, broke me
Broke all my hopes of glee
Snatched my smile from me
And my ability to feel glee

I cried so hard that day
And each day after that day
And even today
It does hurt in some way

I might say
I've healed away
But somewhere, I know
There's still a long way to go

And that it still hurts on some days
In innumerable ways
So much that it almost kills me as I cry
But never lets me die

I know it won't do so
Because it can't do so
But you had the power to
Not cut me through

To not hurt me
To not break me
To not shatter me
To not kill my glee

You had every reason to
But that didn't stop you
From doing it all
From making me fall

Making my confidence fall
Making my belief fall
Making my love feel so low
That it didn't matter if it did go

But it was known to you
That it wasn't true
My love was much above you
And it's still much above you

Because I forgive you
Just as I used to
Even when I loved you
And now that I've fallen out of love with you

...

54

I thought I couldn't be
Away from thee
That I couldn't do
Without you

And now, look at me
So far from thee
Yet not a single day
When I miss you in any way

I'm happy
The way I've never happy
So free
So full of glee

Content with being me
And not trying to be
What you wanted me to be
What you wanted in me

And yet, never being enough
Always lacking in some stuff
Always fall short
Even when you were the one falling short

Yet love never let me see
That you never deserved me
And that I deserved better than thee
For a human being like me

I was better than you
And am still better than you
In every department possible
In every way plausible

Maybe that's why
You made me cry
To hide your insecurities
You built in me, the same insecurities

But it doesn't matter anymore
You don't matter anymore
You're simply a past story
A half forgotten memory

55
The rose petals have dried
My eyes have cried
More than they needed to
More than you deserved to

But it's finally over now
There's nothing left now
Nothing but memories
And bittersweet stories

Memories of love
Of being the one who does love
Who breathes love
Who lives love

Of being the one you never saw
For you, she was full of flaw
Never good enough to be
Even be seen by thee

And yet she loved you
More than you deserved to
More than she could
More than one should

But her love was never supposed to be
What love is normally seen to be
For she didn't just love you
She lived in her love for you

These things might seem to you
Just as confusing as they used to
And trust me
I expect exactly that from thee

I tried my best to
Show my love to you
But you never saw it
And you hated it

And now, you come to me
Ask me
To explain my love for you
To explain what I felt for you

I know you're not asking me
About my love for thee
But asking about someone else's love
If she is the one you love

But I don't have answers for you
My love wasn't meant for you
Not to be taken by you
Not to be given by you

My love was the sea
The depths of which you could never see
For you never did strive
To go ahead and dive

You just wanted the sand
The shore's sand
And that's exactly how it is
That's how your love is

And that's the way it'll always be
That's the most love from thee
Because that's the most you can give
The most you can forgive

You're not me
You'll never be
To be able to
Almost give up myself for you

56
I've done enough
And now I've had enough
Of being taken for granted
Of being unwanted

Of being made replaceable
When you said I was irreplaceable
Of being strong for too long
Of being neglected for so long

I'm tired of being
The one who's dealing
The one who's taunted all day
The one who is never good enough in any way

I'm tired of being the one
Who can never get anything done
As you expect me to do
I'm tired of these unrealistic expectations from you

I can't do
What I can't do
And you always knew
What I couldn't do

Then why do you
Expect me to be able to
Even be able to do
What we both know I can never do?

I can't be one of those dolls
Who have nothing but walls
Nothing but external beauty
Nothing called an entity

I can't be
The one attracting thee
With my body and winks
And those dramatic blinks

I simply don't have the time to
Or the willingness to
If you have to be with me
You need to love me for me

And I don't think you'll be able to
Love me as I love you
Because I've tried enough
And I've had enough

I'm going now, I have to
I can no more be with you
It simply isn't worth my love
For you to misuse my love

57

All that feeling of pain
Has been washed away by disdain
Though I miss you to this day
I don't want you to come my way

It has rained tears on my heart
When we did part
I had to suffer all the pain
Which has now turned into disdain

You never did care and you still don't do
I wish I'd never loved you
It gave me pain and only so
It made me feel so very low

It's so hard to be the same again
For one does change out of so much pain
Love wasn't easy, but it wasn't a game
And playing with my heart was a game so lame

I don't hate you because I cannot
But trust me, I did want to give us one last shot
But your girlfriends came in the way
And us could not exist for even a day

It's hard to think of a life without you
But I'm going to free myself from you
You're toxic and I know it now
And you played me so well, Wow!

I believed you truly loved me
But all you did was to use me
Because I was what you wanted to flaunt
Not the one you want

It wasn't easy and it isn't easy now
But I'm going to free myself from you
I'm going to let go and walk away
And never turn back to look your way

Your name still gives me chills
Smiles come to me when I look at those stills
Of a time when I thought us existed
A time so lovingly wasted

I wish I could erase your memories
And forget all those stories
Of a life I dreamt to love with you
But I have to start anew

I need to start again
And let that pain give gain
I know it isn't the easiest thing to do
But I'm going to do it for me and you

Being a strong girl is so much effort
When you have pain surrounding your fort
I'm going to win this war
Because I didn't fight to lose this war

It's not between you and me
It's between my disdain and my glee
And I'm not going to let disdain win
It's going to be glee all in

Good bye forever
I'm not going to look back, never
It's going to be tough, I know
But this is what I need, we know

58
It's easy to hurt
And you know that well
It's difficult to overcome that hurt
And I know that well

You never cared and you never will
I cared and I wish I stopped it
You hated me and you wished to kill
I hopelessly loved and loved all your shit

I wish I'd known better
But you wish I hadn't
And my love made you the getter
I wish I'd stopped it, but I couldn't

Love made me a slave
And you the master
It threw my happiness in a dark cave
And you were its blaster

I know it now and I hate love
You'd known it always and you loved being the master
You are the reason I can never again love
Just like broken bones never completely heal by plaster

59

I wish I'd never known you
So I wouldn't have fallen for you
I wish we hadn't crossed paths
Such wouldn't have been the aftermaths

We were never mean to be
At least, that's what you thought of me
And my love, you called it infatuation
And took advantage of the entire situation

You used me to be popular
And you made me unpopular
Well, you didn't care
For you had girlfriends to take care

Playboy, cheat, whatever I call you
It can reduce the pain's blue
It just hurts to have loved someone
Who just used you for fun

I'm glad I saw through it
I don't know how deep I would've been in depression's pit
I'm thankful to my idiots for making me aware
That you never did care

I can't love anyone like I loved you
But that won't stop me from starting anew
I'm going to rise from what you made of me
So high and so much full of glee

You'll remember me someday
And that will be the day
That you will realise that the loss was yours and not mine
You lost someone whose love for you did shine

That shine will turn into a dismal sheen
And you will not know how to clean
For some places in one's heart
Once broken, always stay apart

60
You destroyed my today
You couldn't destroy my tomorrow
That better tomorrow became my today
And I'll have more brilliant tomorrows

You killed my happiness
But you couldn't destroy my sorrows
Finally, I have my happiness
And barely any sorrows

I know you wanted me to die
Out of pain and anger
But I'm going to fly
I've made energy out of that anger

I'll be who my mother wanted me to be
I'll be smiling with all my heart
I'll finally be free
My heart will have re-joined all the part

You'll come back to me, I'm sure
When you see what I've become
But I will not be your ego's cure
So distant, I will have become

Love is not a joke, nor is it a game
It's an emotion, and you ought to be true
You can't make a stone out of a gem
Thanks for the heartbreak, it makes me a better person, someone anew

61

I wish I could forget you
And get rid of all that love that I have for you
I wish I saw nothing when I looked back
Instead of the love that you made me lack

Loving you didn't complete me
You didn't let me be
Who I was, who I wanted to be
You killed my dreams and you drained me

I wish I could never see you again
For that fills me up with so much pain
And more than pain, there is disdain
My love for you became my favourite bane

All I craved for was you and you alone
I walked the path of love on my own
You tricked me to believe that you were there with me
And that you were not caging me but setting me free

I wish I'd known it a bit sooner
You were my love's ruiner
You didn't want me to love you anymore
For that wasn't bringing you fame anymore

Was my love just your way to get fame?
Did my love for you look like a game?
I didn't know I was so easy to play with
To deceive and to call my love a myth

You were all that I had
And all that made me sad
I wish I'd known it sooner
That you were my love's ruiner

62

I was like a pearl
So precious a girl
But I was merely a part of the string
Of your many a fling

You didn't look at me as if we had a future
But for me, you were my suture
My cure for all my pain
But for you, I was a game plain

You didn't bother to look back
For me, it was difficult resisting staying back
But I had to move on
Since you were long gone

I'm not going to stop looking back
Merely because it's you that I lack
But that won't stop me from moving ahead
Till I drop dead

I will be a broken person
But not an unsuccessful person
I may be sad on the inside
But I'll never let you know on the outside

You will never have the pleasure of having broken me
For I will never let you have that glee
I will never forget, nor will I forgive
But I promise that those moments, I won't relive

63

I loved you
I still do
And I will continue to
Till life courses me through

Till there's life in me
In my heart will always be
You and only you
I'll always love you

I don't think
You'll even blink
And give a moment of thought
To my world distraught

By loving a man who would never be
The one who loves me
Who'll never even see
What has become of me

Who'll never look my way
Who wasn't mine yesterday
And is not today
And will not be mine on any day

And yet, I will love you
Just as I do
Maybe a little more
Maybe keep you a little closer to my core

You might not love me
But you don't even hate me
You let me be
Simply in love with thee

Maybe you don't know
Or maybe you do know
Either way
You never come in my love's way

You let me be
Let me love thee
Just as I want to
Just as I wish to

That's enough for me
And will always be
That you let me love you
The way I want to

64

All my dreams on the floor
Shown the way to the door
Shattered away
They hurt even today

Maybe it wasn't to be
The way I wanted it to be
Maybe you weren't to be
The man who loved me

I understand that could be
Despite my love for thee
But the least you could do
Was not misuse my love for you?

Not kill me
Without really killing me
Not making me cry
Just because I wanted to try

Try to be
The one loved by thee
Try to be good enough for you
To be the one for you

You might have never loved me
You didn't even need to hate me
You didn't need to fill me up with pain
Fill each cell with disdain

I might have walked away
But the hurt does stay
And it probably does so
Till the world has even an ounce of sorrow

Or till I am to be
Whoever is me
To be a human being
Who is but a bundle of feeling

Till death do us apart
The hurt will always be a part
Of my inner core
Even if I don't love you anymore

I might not be able to
Be loved by you
But this hurt will always remind me
Why I am better off without thee

Why I needed to go
Why my tears needed to flow
For one last time
In this lifetime

Why I needed to
Let go of my love for you
Why I needed to
Not love you

65
When you rejected me
You made me a better me
You taught me to
Look ahead of you

To look at me
And see all I could be
See all I could be
If I wanted to be

You showed me
How to be me
How to love me
And not just love thee

You never belittled me
For having loved thee
For being the rejected one
For being the not-good-enough one

Instead
You led
You led me to see
What I could be

How far I could go
How ahead I should go
Because I had it in me
Which I could never see

But you could see
And you believed in me
As I had never done
And would have never done

Had it not been for you
For my rejection from you
And the friendship that grew
From that rejection from you

You never saw me
As a partner for thee
But you saw in me
What no one else could see

Or maybe
They could see
But didn't tell me
So that I couldn't be

What I deserved to be
What I could be
You saw my potential there
And raised it with care

I thank you today
For rejecting me that day
For showing me the way
Each day, in a new way

66
You ended me entire
Set my soul on fire
And left me
To be

You just never thought
Of that battles I'd fought
For you
Only for you

You never saw
How I ignored each flaw
And how you
Never let my love through

How you always did ignore
My love, each time, all the more
And yet I kept on loving you
No matter what you do

You thought I was weak?
My heart was meek?
That I'd die
No matter how much I try?

You don't know
And you'll never even know
That the love in me
Is greater than any pain you give me

It'll always heal me
No matter what I get from thee
I never burnt to ashes
You couldn't even harm my eyelashes

The fire you set on me
Was only hot to thee
It never touched me
Never harmed me

It never would
For it never could
Love was there for me
Within me

No fire, no ice
None of your Vice
Nothing could ever do to me
What you wanted to happen to me

All I learnt was
Loving you was a lost cause
I might not love you anymore
But I still hold love to my core

67

I might never know
But you do know
Why you hurt me
Why you mistreated me

Why you never understood me
Why you never tried to understand me
Why I was never enough for you
No matter how much my love for you

Why I was
Always the lost cause
The one you never saw
The one that was but a flaw

The one whose love was
Never a sufficient cause
Whose love would never be
Even be replied to with a smile from thee

I understand you never loved me
You couldn't love me
I understand that to be
But I still don't understand thee

I don't understand why
You made me cry
You made me fearful
My eyes tearful

When all I did was to
Endlessly love you
Do everything I could do
For you

When my love was true
Why wasn't it enough for you?
To at least not mistreat me?
To not ignore me?

You could have simply spoken to me
Told me you didn't love me
Made it clear to me
That you wouldn't love me

Why did you make me suffer endlessly?
Why did you make me live painfully?
Was that necessary
I don't think it was to be

Anyway
All I have to say
Is that I forgive you
For all you made me go through

For all the pain
That I had to go through in vain
All the hurt in me
That doesn't let me be

I forgive you
And release you
From within me
From within my love for thee

I don't love you
And I will never do
It might still hurt on some day
But I'll manage it some way

68
I couldn't be
Enough for thee
No matter how much I tried to be
It simply wasn't meant to be

It really was not
And yet I fought
Maybe, it might be
Why not, was all that was within me

Maybe that hope
That endless hope
Maybe that hurts today
In a different way

Maybe it hurts to
Simply not have you
Not be there
To give you love and care

I never expected you to
Love me, too
All I wanted from you
Was to see my love for you

To recognize it
To believe it
And not just think
That I wanted to have a link

I wasn't looking for that
I'm still not looking for that
There might be many girls who do
Want to have a link with you

For you're rich
But so am I rich
Richer than you
Much richer than you

Maybe you never saw so
Just as you never saw my sorrow
My pain, my hurt
All of which I suffered in vain

Today, when I look back
I see all that I lack
The smile that used to be
So characteristic of me

I lost it to you
To the pain you made me go through
To the extent that now
It won't come anyhow

I wish I could go back to me
And tell her to smile despite thee
Despite what you made her go through
She was always enough for you

Even if you couldn't see it
Couldn't feel it
Or that you hid it
So you didn't have to face it

Either way
She was better than you in each way
I'd tell her she was enough
No matter how you made her life tough

69

Each time I care
I'm met with despair
Each time I love you
You push me away from you

You prove to me
That you don't want me
You never wanted me
And that you'll never want me

I could never be
What was wanted by thee
I would always be
The one undesired by thee

The one you could easily do without
The one you showed the way out
Out of your life
And yet, not out of your life

I'm still here
And you've kept me here
I did go away
But you brought me back one day

I decided to stay
And not love anyway
But each time it happens again
When you speak to me again

When you look at me
When you care for me
When you talk to me
Of things about thee

Even if it's your girlfriend
Or your closest friend
You make me feel loved
Even when I know I'm anything but loved

70
I could never tell you
That I loved you
Nor can I today
When I don't love you in any way

I'm not ashamed that I did
I'm not ashamed that I hid
Somewhere I know in my heart
That was the best part

Had you known about my love for you
I wouldn't have had this bond with you
Wouldn't have been able to be
The confidant you see in me

Maybe I wasn't able to
See the same love in you
Maybe I never saw so
For it was never so

And I believe the second one
It seems like the more real one
Why would you love me
When even I didn't love me?

When even I never saw anything in me
How would you be able to see
Anything in me
That would make you love me?

I am not that person anymore
Nor do I love you anymore
But somewhere in me
Still lies a soft corner for thee

And no matter where I be
That'll always be
For they rightly say
Love doesn't really go away

71
You cut my wings
With all those small little things
All those little things
That brought in the negative feelings

Like looking away
Each single day
Never looking at me
Even if I was standing next to thee

Not speaking to me
No matter what be
Even if I came to meet you
Even if I risked it all to speak to you

Coming over here
To take her over there
To show me
That you were better off without me

That I wasn't enough
And I would never be enough
No matter what I did do
I wouldn't be enough for you

For I was a living flaw
And you hated me as a law
You would simply get rid of me
If it were up to thee

You broke me
With all you did to me
You hated me
For loving thee

You shattered my heart
Into a million part
All scattered on the floor
As you showed me the door

I never was told
That this is what lobe would hold
For me, or for anyone it might be
I never knew this is what love would do to me

It made me so weak
So meek
That I never said anything
And faced everything

I never saw
A single flaw
In you back then
Even when you were the worst of men

Yet, I loved you
I almost worshipped you
And even then, you broke me
Does it haunt you, what you did to me?

Do you ever feel guilty for doing so?
For making me suffer so?
For mistreating me?
For breaking me?

72
You broke my heart
Into a million part
From the very start
As if like a work of art

Maybe you didn't want to
Didn't intend to
Maybe you didn't really care
About my love and care

Maybe you couldn't see
What was in me
All those feelings for you
All my dreams, which I saw of being with you

Maybe you simply could not
Or would not
I don't blame you today
Just as I didn't even that day

When you told me
You were leaving me
And going away
And would never come back to stay

You would never be
With someone like me
With someone who
Was me to you

It hurt that day
It still hurts till this day
There are still nights
When my heart still fights

For you to be
With me
To understand me
To understand my love for thee

But my soul knows that it will never be
It simply can't be
You're happy with her
In love with her

Maybe she's the one for you
The one I could never be for you
Maybe it simply wasn't meant to be
The love between you and me

73
I've forgiven you
And it's time you do, too
You've been unjust with me
Is the least I have to say to thee

Yet, I don't want to
Hold it against you
And I won't do so
I'm over my sorrow

And I hope you find a way
To get over your guilt one day
If you do have any
Reasons for that seem to be many

I'm not here to show them to you
Or to taunt you
All I'm trying to say
Is that I hope you can forgive yourself one day

For all you did to me
All you made of me
For I've walked on
Moved on

And I hope you find the strength to
Do the same, too
To learn from the past
And walk past

74

I look at you again
Despite the pain
And the lack of it
Yet, my soul doesn't hit

It doesn't question me
It doesn't speak of thee
Doesn't say it hurts to
See anything about you

I wonder how
I did allow
Yourself to affect me
To the point of destroying me

And it wasn't you
Who tried to
It was me
Who was destroying me

I don't know if you saw so
My eyes full of sorrow
My soul screaming in pain
Which now seems to be in vain

Because now, when I look at you
I don't feel anything for you
Nothing at all, and it's something new
I've never felt nothing for you

75

I wonder tonight
Of all that plight
All I went through
Because of you

I see myself there
And you're also there
I look at it again and again
But, in vain

I already know
What I do know
And the part I'm looking for in it
Is not a part of it

I'm still looking for a reason to forgive you
A reason for all you did do
A cause
That deserves applause

A reason why
You made me cry
Except for the fact that
Sadistry was what was under your hat

That you found yourself happy
By making me unhappy
I still look back again
But, alas, in vain

76
You ignore me
Speak over me
Hear everyone but me
And yet you ask me

Where you went wrong?
Why we weren't together all along?
Why I don't love you anymore
Like I used to, from the very core?

You ask me
As shamelessly as can be
And I don't know what to say
Even today

Just like I didn't know
What was to follow
When I began loving you
I didn't know what I was signing up to

But thank you
For all I went through
For all you taught me
And for all you took away from me

Somewhere, I see
I needed thee
To be able to be
This version of me

77
While I cried
A part of me died
And you couldn't see
That I died for thee

Maybe your eyes
Couldn't see my lies
Couldn't see my pain
My tearful stain

Which was there on my t-shirt
Screaming my hurt
You were there, too
But it was invisible to you

I was scared of what I'd say
Had you asked about it that day
But I forgot something
For you, I was nothing

You didn't care
Didn't even pretend to care
All you did was ignore
And show me I was a bore

I don't know what to even say to you
For all you've made me go through
Because even that'd make me fall for you again
And add to my never-ending pain

78
I wonder why
I still do cry
When I seem to
Have moved on from you

From the love I had for you
The importance of you
The reason I used to
Live, was sometimes you

And today, none of it is so
Then why the sorrow
Why do the memories come back again
And reignite the pain?

You're not coming back
Nor do I anymore lack
In anything, that you could complete
Then why this painful feat?

Why do I have to go through
All the pain because of you?
Haven't I suffered enough already
Haven't you hurt me enough already?

79
I try my best to
Not cry for you
And yet each day
You find a new way

Into my deepest fears
And then, to my tears
You make me feel
Like I'm never going to heal

And trust me
I do fall for these words of thee
On my bad days
In more than one ways

But then, I remember why
I wanted to try
To get over you
To move on from you

And that helps me
Gives strength to me
Tells me why
I do cry

It's because I'm true
About my feelings for you
And that truth hurts on some days
In more than one ways

80
Today
When you came my way
When we spoke again
There was a strange pain

The thought
That my mind fought
Was why and how
I didn't feel anything somehow

As cold as ice I felt
A void inside of me, I dealt
I wonder how it was there
And why it was there

Was it because I didn't love you anymore
Or that I'd run out of love's store?
Was it because I was tired of you
And all the baggage that came with you?

I don't know
I doubt I'll ever know
All I know for now is
This state is but a painful bliss

81

Each morning I wake up to see
Nothing has changed between you and me
How I wish it wasn't so
That there was something but sorrow

Maybe it isn't that way
When you look at me today
Probably on your side, even today
The sun still brightens your day

Maybe it is just me
And my feelings for thee
That refuse to go away
And haunt me each day

Each day, there's something new
About my feelings for you
The more I try to let go
The more love does flow

And it does hurt to see
You not even considering me
Worthy of being loved by you
For probably, you don't know that I do love you

82

I question my plight
Each and every night
If it's actually there
Or if it's just in here

Inside my heart
My broken heart
It wasn't like this in the start
Wasn't broken into a million part

It wasn't this way
And I never thought it'd be this way
Never did it occur to me
That it'd ever be

That you'd hurt me
Break me
Belittle me
Curse me

While I'd just stand there
And just stare
Not being able to
Understand what to say to you

Not being able to
Understand you
Understand why you would want to
Hurt someone who loves you

I still don't
And I probably won't
Understand why you did so
Why you filled my sleepless nights with sorrow

83

Each time I look at you
My heart calls out to you
No matter how much I hush it
Nothing ever changes it

It still beats for you
Still loves you
Despite the fact that I've explained why
We'll never be together, no matter how much it does cry

No matter my tears
My fears
My pain
It'll all be in vain

Yet, it still goes on
From dusk to dawn
And again
And again

As if there's nothing else to do
But to love you
Despite the knowledge that you'll never love me
Irrespective of whether I love thee

I'm tired of being hurt every day
When you don't look at me the way
In which I look at you
I don't see love in you

At least not for me
Maybe someone else is loved by thee
And all I can say
For your happiness will I pray

84

Whenever I speak to you
I fall for you
Even though I try my best not to
For it'll never be that way for you

And I'm tired of hurting myself
For loving thyself
For each time you speak of her that way
You break my heart away

Despite the fact that you're not together anymore
She's still a part of your core
And she'll probably always be
Where I'll never be

You won't ever see
Anything in me
You will never be
The man who loves me

And while I accept it so
It still brings me sorrow
It is natural to
For I still love you

I've tried so hard to
Move on from you
But each time I speak to
I fall in love with you

85

I still don't know why
But I do cry
On some days, like today
When love just doesn't know another way

No other place to go
Except my sorrow
For each time you speak to me
I realise you'll never love me

And yet, no matter what I do
I can't seem to get over you
Over this love
Which I can't seem to unlove

I don't know how long I can go
Just hiding this sorrow
And smiling away
Each and every single day

Don't blame me
If I break down in front of thee
While I might never say a thing
It'll just be a flooding of feeling

I don't know how to
Stop myself from loving you
Or how to make you
Fall for me, too

And that gap keeps killing me
Keeps hurting me
Doesn't let me sleep
Makes me weep

And I'm tired of being a part
Of the pain of the heart
But then, it's my heart and I'll have to bear
The pain of my love and care

86
Each time I miss you
I wonder if I really do
Is it you that I miss
Or a piece of me amiss?

Is it the love I saw in you
And still do
The one you couldn't find in me
But found in 'she'

I don't blame you
Nor do I want to hurt you
So I'll never tell you
That I do love you

That'll only hurt you more
Maybe all the way up to the core
And while you're already broken
I can't be the reason your world is shaken

You do speak to me
Sometimes even notice me
Smile at me on some days
That all I need, my heart says

Maybe that's what love is
A painful bliss
And yet we choose to be
In love, like I am, with thee

87

Why do I look at thee
The way you'll never look at me?
Why do I think of thee
When I know you'll never think of me?

Why do I do
Everything that I do
In a hope for you
In my love for you?

Why do I see
Daydreams of thee
When I clearly know
There's nothing to follow?

You're not mine and never will you be
Nor do I even hope for you to be
Yet, why do I
Unendingly try?

Try to be 'she'
The one loved by thee
Daydream about you
More than I could ever tell you

Each night I weep
Before I sleep
Because it hurts to
Love you when I know you'll never love me, too

88

I wonder what I see
Each time I look at thee
That makes me feel so happy
Like I've never been so happy

I don't know
What is to follow
But from where I see
I don't think you'll ever love me

And yet, I do
Keep on loving you
Keep on trying to be
That version of me

The one you can love
Like I do love
This very version of you
And every other version of you

For reason I can't seem to know
Or the consequences I can't seem to follow
But all I know for today
Is that I love you in every way

And the realisation for me
Is that you don't love me
And probably never will
At least out of your own will

89

It was never unknown to me
That you didn't love me
And yet, I don't know why
I did try

I tried hard
Very hard
To be worthy
Of thee

To be the one for you
The one loved by you
At least seen by you
Noticed by you

But no matter how hard I tried
Each night, I cried
For every day seemed to be
Worse than the day behind me

And it hurt to be
The one loving thee
So very much
That the wounds hurt to touch

90
I wonder if you think of me
If I ever mattered to thee
If you even thought about me
Before hurting me

Before you killed me
Yet didn't kill me
You made me suffer again and again
From an endless pain

Why?
Because I did try?
Because I wanted to
Honestly love you?

Because I was fair
In a game unfair?
Because I loved you
More than I knew I could do?

And in that love, I gave you
The right to kill me all through
Trusting you not to
Hurt me all through

And you did exactly that to me
You broke me
Shattered my dreams
Threw the pieces across realms

You tried your best to
Stop me from loving you
Was love really such a wrong thing to do
For which so much pain I was to go through?

91

I don't know why I do
Still wait for you
When I know today
That you'll never come this way

For you know, too
That I'm waiting for you
Looking out for you
Just to meet you

And maybe
You don't want to hurt me
By telling me
That you don't love me

But trust me
I know thee
And this is something I've known
Ever since the seed of love has been sown

I always knew
That you'll never love me, too
And yet, like a fool
I still drool

Not physically
But mentally
And I'm not ashamed to
Admit that I love you

And I love you
Knowing very well that you'll never love me, too
And trust me, it doesn't affect my love for you
For my love isn't a question that needs an answer from you

92

Each night I try
Not to cry
Not to break down
Not to end the day with a frown

And yet, I fail
For the heart is frail
And it hurts to
Not be loved by you

Even though I know why
I do cry
For reasons are for the brain
Giving them to the heart is in vain

For it's not meant to
Understand things anew
It's just meant to
Go on loving you

And it asks me
"Is it too much to ask of thee
To love me
Just as I love thee?"

93
I fall in love with you again
Knowing it'll be in vain
That there'll never be
Anything like my idea of 'we'

And yet, no matter how much I try
No matter how much I beg and cry
The heart doesn't seem to listen to me
When it comes to thee

It's rigid there
For your care
For you make me feel
Like I've always wanted to feel

But I know
That it's just the flow
And that there are no feelings there
Behind your care

You make me laugh like I never have
Make me smile like I never have
Make me feel so good
Make me feel understood

And yet, you don't feel for me
And look at me
Unable to stop myself
From falling for thyself

I know for a fact so
That it'll only lead to sorrow
Yet, I can't find a way
To love you any less today

94
In the light
Of the bright sunlight
I remember that day
When I laughed my heart away

I never knew
I had seriously no clue
That I could laugh so much
That my belly would hurt to touch

But you made sure of so
You almost stole all my woe
And I know that you don't love me
Nor will I ever expect that of thee

Honestly, even I wasn't expecting to be
So much in love with thee
But it happened, somewhere along the way
And I realised it today

Trust me, I'm trying my best to
Get rid of these feelings for you
For I know
That it'd bring nothing but woe

And the friendship we have today
Is the most cherished thing I have today
I don't want to lose it to
The feelings I have for you

95
It's scary to see
You talk to me
For I don't know when my heart
Will be shattered into a million part

You might say
Something today
That would break me
More than could ever be known to me

And yet I do
Talk to you
For something there
Feels like love and care

But I do know
I'm too low
For you to
Ever give love to

There are hundreds there
At whom you stare
About whom you drool
Like a fool

And one of them will be
The one loved by thee
She'll love you, too
The way I did, too

You'll never know
The story of my woe
For I'll always be
Just a friend to thee

96

I wonder why
I do cry
Each night for you
Yearning for you

When you don't even see
Anything in me
To even be
Able to speak to me

I'm so uninteresting to you
So vestigial for you
Yet, why is it so
That your walking away fills me with woe?

While I know in a way
That we'll meet each day
And tomorrow is just one
When the same cycle will be done

You'll meet me
Speak to me
And go away
Like you did yesterday

It'll not mean anything to you
But I'll spend all night thinking of you
Thinking of each word you said
And each word you left unsaid

And wait till the next day
For the cycle to repeat away
Knowing very well that there'll never be
Anything like my idea of 'we'

97

I wonder why it's necessary
For this story
To always be
Just a story?

Just a dream that I see
That involves me
And thee
And the idea of 'we'

Why can't it be that way
Each and every day
The way I see
Each time I think of thee?

It doesn't cost to dream, they say
But my heart breaks every day
Each time I see or meet you
I realise it'll never be true

It hurts to be
So much in love with thee
And never be able to see
Anything in your eyes for me

It hurts to be here
To be the only one to care
To be the only one who dreams away
Every single night and day

98

I wish I knew
What it was to love you
I wish I knew
What would come out of my love for you

You'd never love me
Was always known to me
But that you'd hate me
Was something I never expected of thee

I don't know why
I still do cry
When it should be you
Whose eyes have tears anew

I wasn't wrong
In loving you all along
I would've accepted it upright
If there was anything that wasn't right

Love isn't wrong
Never can loving someone be wrong
But just because I cared for you
Didn't mean I was a slave to you

But you treated me so
And I accepted the sorrow
All out of care
In my heart, that was there

But I wonder how
You could allow
Yourself to do
All you did do

Doesn't your conscience prick you?
Don't the nights haunt you?
Does it ever occur to you
What you made me go through?

Do you ever question yourself
Of what you did to my self?
Of what you did so
Why you made me go through sorrow?

99
I wish there was
A plausible cause
Why you chose to
Hurt me all through

But from where I see
As far as I can see
There seems to be
No cause for thee

To hurt me
To blame me
To belittle me
To crush me

To break my dreams away
To break my heart everyday
To break me so much
That my soul still hurts to touch

I don't see why
You made me cry
So much each day
In some or the other way

100
I bleed poetry
To get rid of thee
To throw you away
From my system each day

But somehow you do
Find a new way through
Back into my system every day
No matter how far I throw you away

And it strikes me
Is it thee
Or the love I have for thee
That I push out of me?

For if it were you
It'd not come back to me anew
It'd throw me away
Not be thrown away each day

Maybe it's not you
But the love I have for you
Whatever be it so
It does bring me sorrow

And somewhere, it is you
For it was you
Who hurt me all through
Who's responsible for the pain I went through

I wish I could say
Something good today
But what do I say
To the one because of whom I hurt every day?

101
I wish I could unlove you
Somehow remove you
From the recesses of my memory
Where lies our story

A story no one knows
A story that still flows
In the midst of silence
It still causes violence

Both our hearts
It breaks into parts
And yet we both choose to
Not speak of it all through

You might be silent
But your heart is violent
I know it so
How? Don't ask me so

You tell me that
I can see what you hide in your hat
I know it hurts to
Not be able to love me as I love you

But don't you worry
It's still a valid story
Even if it's just me
Loving thee

And not receiving any love
In return to my love
It's still just as true
As it would be had you loved me, too

102
I wish I could forget you
And start life anew
But each time I try to
You waltz into my life anew

And somehow, that makes me weak
Makes the intention bleak
And I end up going with the flow
And feeling all the more low

I see
What you don't see
What you'll never see
I see love in thee

The one you keep locked up inside
The one you want to hide
I see it there
As if it was just bare

I see you still love her
Even though you'll never admit to her
And somewhere, I feel
It's the same that we both feel

But then, we don't
And we won't
For you want to be with her again
And I just accept my pain

I know
That it's an unending woe
My love for you
That's all it is, all through

For you'll never love me
And I'll not be able to unlove thee
A stalemate, it is
A painful bliss

103
Would you ever love me like I love you?
Would you ever see in me what I see in you?
Would you ever dare to care like I do?
Would you ever dare to bare you heart like I do?

A hundred such questions arise
So do a hundred beautiful lies
Each time I ask myself
Regarding thy self

If I deserve you
If I deserve to be with you
If I deserve to see
The entire world, with thee

But then, a whisper is there
Which leaves my heart bare
And all I can do
Is stare at the picture of you

It asks me
If you deserve me
If you deserve all the love and care
If loving you even is fair?

If you are worthy of all this
Of the beautiful bliss
That I try to
Create for you

And each time
Like every previous time
I have no response to say
But I do know the answer each day

104
Each time I look at you
I wonder anew
What I see in you
That makes me love you

Why I feel
All that I feel
When you feel nothing
In return for my everything

And never will you do
Feel anything like I do
At least for me
About that, I'm sure of thee

That you'll never love me
No matter how much I love thee
No matter how much I care
All I'll be ever be met with is despair

And no matter how much I try
No matter how many nights I cry
I'll still have to wake up to be
Still a nothing to thee

105

I wish there was a way
To unlove you today
To look at you
And not feel anything for you

Or maybe something
That's not this love thing
Something different
Like you're so indifferent

I'd like to be there
To not care
To not give a damn
To call love a sham

To have myself closed away
To love her everyday
To grieve the breakup everyday
To ignore me everyday

Somewhere, I'd like to see
What you see
How you live each day
How you never see my way

While I can't see
Anything but thee
You never seem to
Take any notice of me all through

Maybe because
Of all I was
And all I'll ever be
Will never be for thee

Maybe we're not meant to be
Even though I love thee
Not because fate said so
But because there's too much sorrow

And to be able to
Go on loving you
In the midst of this sea
Seems impossible to be

Yet, I do try each day
In some of the other way
But I know this, too
That I'll never make it through

Somewhere inside of me
It hurts to be loving thee
When I know clearly
That you'll never even think of being in love with me

106

I look back to see
To find where I fell short for thee
I find nothing yet again
And that's what brings me pain

If only there was a reason
Why love never had a season
If only there was a day
When I could pinpoint in my way

But then, I tell myself
Maybe I'm biased for my self
And against you
For not loving me, too

But somewhere I know
I couldn't fall so low
I've always been so harsh on myself
I could never be partial to myself

And especially when it came to you
So much is the love for you
There was nothing I see
In which I don't see thee

And yet again today
I don't find a way
To become that version of me
That can be lovable to thee

That's what hurts me
Each time I look at thee
And you don't look at me
The way I look at thee

107
I wish I could tell you
What I feel for you
And hope somehow that you
Would say the same, too

But neither of the two
Is ever going to happen between me and you
Neither do I have the courage to admit my love for you
Nor an expectation for you to love me, too

It'd be too unrealistic to
Expect that of you
When I clearly know
Of your woe

Of how broken you are
Yet, you look all calm from afar
It's only when one sees you from close
Does one find these woes

Thank you
For letting me through
To those closed recesses of your soul
For showing me the deepest part of your soul

But I wonder how it felt for you
To go through all that anew
Did it hurt again?
Did it remind you of the pain?

Before I had a chance to ask
You left me with the task
Of collecting myself back again
And never speaking of it again

It was unsaid between us
And so will it remain thus
I'll never tell anyone anything
And you, will probably never say anything

108

Depths we've seen together
And yet we seem not to know each other
It's funny how it is so
How fate could fall so low

You were the one to bare
All your heart out there
And yet, somehow, it's me
Who fell in love with thee

It should've clearly been the other way
Than it is today
But then, who can say
What happens today?

There's no expectation here
For you to care
But somewhere, there still is a hope
That the answer will not be a nope

When I clearly know it is
And yet, that hope still is
Maybe that's how the heart is
Even in the midst of pain, it finds bliss

That's what loving you is
A painful bliss
And yet, each day
I do it again, in a new yet old way

109
There used to be
So much love in me
Each sight of you
Filled me with love anew

And now
I would never allow
Myself to see you
Or willingly meet you

There's nothing I see anymore
Except that you hurt me to the core
Not once, but a million times
More than I could ever hurt you in a million lifetimes

Yet, I went on loving you
And caring for you
And you went on hating me
And hurting me

On some days
I wish we hadn't crossed ways
That I'd never met you
Never known you

I'd have never fallen for you
Had never been hated by you
Had never seen myself
The way you saw my self

But then, I realize
All those tries
Were never to achieve you
But to better my love for you

And somewhere
All that has helped me care
For those I need to
And not waste it on you

I don't hate you
And I will never do
But I will never love you
No matter what I do

110

For some unknown reason
Love's become an unending season
And there seems to be
No way out for me

Each time I try to
Run away from you
Something or the other
Doesn't let my love wither

So much do I cry
So hard do I try
But somewhere, I know
There's nothing coming out of this woe

I can try oceans if I want to
But never will I be lovable to you
Because, for that to happen to me
You'd have to forget 'she'

And that would never be
You'd never forget 'she'
Never think of me
The way I think of thee

Never love me
Never stay up nights for me
Never look at me
The way I look at thee

And endlessly the cycle goes on
My heart stays forlorn
But there never seems to be
Anything new for thee

You keep missing 'she'
I keep loving thee
And this goes on each day
No matter what leave or stay

111
I wonder how long I can go on
Loving you with this heart forlorn
And each time I think so
My heart fills with sorrow

I don't know
If my woe
Is for me
Or for thee

You deserve to be loved
The way you loved
And while that is true
You don't allow anyone to love you

I wonder why you do so
Keep yourself drowned in sorrow
When you clearly know
You deserve more than this woe

I'm not asking you to
Let me love you through
All I'm saying is that you need to
Release the pain you hold so close to you

Not just you
It affects me, too
While I may never say so
Your sadness does cause me sorrow

And me?
Loving thee
Is enough pain
To suffer in vain

For I know clearly
You'll never love me
Yet I can't stop myself
From loving thyself

The two of us undergo pain
All in vain
But at least you have a way
To let it go someday

Let it go
Let go of the woe
You need to do so
If not for yourself, for my sorrow?

112

I saw you as I see God
And you saw me as fraud
I never found why
You made me cry

You broke me all the way to the core
Till there was nothing anymore
Nothing in me
Was about me

Broken pieces everywhere
Yet, a loving stare
You broke me down
While I fixed your frown

Even the thought of your eyes having a tear
Almost killed me with fear
That tear be there because of me
Would be even scarier than the worst nightmare for me

So much did I love you
And yet, it was never enough for you
I wasn't enough for you
Never good enough for you

I wish I could ask you
What you wanted all through
But maybe, I'm better off without the answer
Maybe my heart won't be able to take the answer

113
I feel so blank today
As if I've nothing to say
But my heart explodes
Tired of its loads

Tired of loving you
Tired of caring for you
And yet, never bring able to
Fall out of love with you

Each time I see you
I wonder what I see in you
But somewhere in me
I know it's the love I have for thee

It's not in you, but in me
As to what I see
Each time I see you
That's what makes it special anew

But somewhere in me
The wish to be
The loved one of thee stays
And it hurts these days

114
I had accepted that you'd never love me
The way I love thee
That you'd never see in me
What I see in thee

I had even started to
Walk away from you
Almost started to
Let go of my love for you

But somehow it's there again
Both, the love and the pain
And I don't know what to do
Of all these emotions that I feel for you

Neither do I want to
Embrace them anew
Nor do I want to
Leave me blank like you do

You seem to know
What to do with this woe
Tell me what to do
About these feelings for you

115
Somehow, in some way
On a random day
Maybe tell me again
Of what you do to your pain

Of how you deal with it
Where you hide it
How you hide it
And how you bear it

Does it resurface on some days?
What do you do on those days?
Where do you vent it all
The stories where you fall?

When you fail,
Where do you wail?
On whose shoulder do you cry
When you fail, no matter how hard you try?

Tell me
Teach me
For I need it, too
To deal with my feelings for you

116
As I sit down to write
About my plight
I realise I have nothing to say
Like I did that day

When you taunted me
Belittled me
Those memories still haunt me
They simply don't let me be

Each time I think I've done my healing
Comes back the feeling
That arose each day
When you pushed me away

When you hurt me
Ignored me
Ridiculed me
Laughed at me

And I always forgave you
Out of my love for you
Never realising so
That you were the reason for my sorrow

Never saw you
For you
But for the imagine of you
I'd begin to love anew

Never realised that you were no more
The man I loved from the core
Or that you never were the person I loved
It was always the image I loved

The image was pure
And my love was sure
But so very kind
And exceptionally blind

I never saw you
When you cut me all through
Broke my heart, my dreams, and threw them away
Not once, but you did it each day

And I never said a thing
For I never knew a thing
So blind my love was
So much pain it does cause

But whatever that be
I don't wish to ponder over thee
You never worthy of me
And you will never be

And saying so
I walk away from the sorrow
That was yours to give me
And is mine to not allow anymore from thee

117
I thought you'd complete me
That you'd appreciate me
For being me
For being who I wanted to be

For not being fake to you
For trying to be the one for you
At least I tried to be
Even if I couldn't be

But you never saw anything
All you saw was your feeling
That never let you go away
From that fated day

When she walked away from you
Broke your heart all through
Hurt you in ways you never speak about
In ways that I very well know about

And all I wanted to do
Was to help you
To heal you
To rejuvenate you

To remind you
Of who really are you
Of what you can be
If you decide to believe in glee

But what did you do to me?
Threw me
All across the bay
To never contact you another day

Pushed me so far
Farther than the farthest star
Just because I wanted to
Help you be you?

I didn't even ask for your love
In return for my love
Didn't even ask you to
Understand me, too

Even though it was my right to
Ask of all this from you
For what I was trying to do
Wasn't easy for me, too

But what do I even say
To the man across the bay?
The man who hated me
Just because I loved and cared for thee?

118

I go back to see
Where I messed up with thee
Where I lost you
Where I felt lost, too

I look back trying to find
A fault in the bind
A mistake which cost me
Everything I had with thee

And somehow, even today
Do I find no way
To navigate to that point
Wherefrom bifurcated this joint

Most people still ask me
About the well being of thee
Not realising that while it might never seem so
I'm already dealing with a lot of woe

How do I get over you?
For I never had you
And will never have you
No matter what I say or do

While I've accepted this fate
It haunts me of late
It haunts me to
Simply let go of you

119
I still want to
Try to be the one for you
But each time I want to
I'm reminded of why that would never do

For I could never be
The one and only 'she'
No matter how much I tried to be
She was everything I could ever be

Each night when I try to
Dream of you
My heart tells me
Why you won't love me

I know it's cruel, but it true
You would never love me, too
No matter what I do
I could never be the one for you

But defeat is what I never knew
I had to accept for you
I've never done so before
And I know it'll hurt to the core

Yet, I try each day
Knowing that I fail everyday
Just to postpone the feeling that I've lost you
And that I'll never have you

120
Today draws to an end
Yet the road has no bend
I keep walking
And life keeps talking

Some days, the words hurt
When I pretend to be unhurt
Whatever they be
At least they are true to me

Not like you
Who could never do
This simple task
Truth seemed like too much to ask

Lies and lies it was
For no reasonable cause
If I ask you to tell me why you made me cry
You'd have no words, no matter how hard you try

And still
I do, and possibly will
Continue to
Go on loving you

Not like I have much to do
About my love for you
It seems to have a mind of its own
And a courage that can never be torn

Not just you, but even my own self
Can't break it down within myself
And while I know that to be
I still fight against this love I have for thee

Maybe, there'll be a day
When this unending way
Will take a turn
To a point of no return

121

Each time I see
The clock next to me
It shows me
How close I was to thee

And how close we'll never again be
Adds the voice in me
I still sometimes look back at the memories
Still sometimes tell myself those stories

Of days that went by
Without even a try
We wouldn't even know
Of a feeling called woe

And it has come to be
The central piece in me
So much for loving you
And being true

I still miss thee
Each time I think of thee
But would I want to be
Who I used to be?

That's a question I can't seem to
Think about getting through
While I'd love to be just that happy
But I'm also proud of who I've grown to be

It's still a question that hangs away
Even though it's the hundredth day
Of our parting ways
Just like all the other days

122

I wonder if you think of me
When you are away from me
I wonder if my voice rings in your ears
When you think of your nears and dears

For yours is the first to
Make it through
Before anyone else
It belongs to you, my heart tells

And it says it so innocently
That I forget to remember thee
And that I will never be
The one loved by thee

It's always been her
And it'll always be her
Even though we both know
That's but an empty woe

You might be forlorn
But she's moved on
And there's no way
That she'd come to you any day

But yet, you keep waiting for her
Knowing well it'll never be her
Just like I wait to be loved by you
Knowing full well that you'll never do

123
I loved you
I still do
You didn't love me that day
You don't love me today

All that's new
Is that my love for you?
Which has grown leaps and bounds
It's a beautiful feeling that now surrounds

It used to be
Inside of me
And now it's everywhere
Wherever I can see or stare

I wonder how it can be
The way it envelopes me
It should've never been that way
For you never loved me in any way

And love isn't supposed to grow
In a place so low
In a heart
Who's on its way to be broken into a million part

And yet, I know
No matter what the woe
Those millions parts will still love you
Just like they used to

And no matter what be
We'll always be
What we used to be
With the weight of unsaid on me

124
I look back to see
The younger version of me
So hopelessly in love with you
And yet, who never said a word to you

Not that we didn't speak
But of love, we didn't speak
At least of my love for you
We did speak of the girls loved by you

And like a friend should do
I consoled you
Each time you broke up
I tried to cheer you up

That was always my love language
Which never seemed to be your language
Maybe beauty and makeup were your languages
Which have always seemed to me as cryptic languages

Whatever that may be
That's for the younger me
But when I look at you today
Why do I feel like talking to you each day?

Why do I see
In everything I see
And even in me,
Some part of thee?

Why has it become of me
To try to find thee
In everything that happens to be
Existing nearby me?

They tell me
That I love thee
But I don't want to
Even think of loving you

For I know clearly
You'll never love me
And I'm not interested in being
The only one who's falling

I've done that before
And it hurt to the core
I don't wish to do
The same anew
125
On some days
We do cross ways
And it is not me
Who is ashamed of seeing thee

But it is thee
Whose eyes lower when you see me
Not of respect for me
But of the guilt in thee

While my eyes stay
Focused on the way
For I know
I'd never been low

All I did was in love
All I had was love
All I saw was in love
All I spoke was for love

And when you see

Things from where I see
You'd see for yourself
Why I'm proud of myself

Proud of who I am today
Who I was yesterday
And regarding tomorrow
I hold no sorrow

But when we come to you
The guilt kills you
It haunts you each night
Of my plight

Of what you did to me
Just because I loved thee
Just because I was so sure
Of my love so pure

Despite all you did to me
I do pray for thee
For you to find peace someday
To find strength to face your guilt one day

126
I'm tired of feeling
Pretty much everything
Tired of being
The only one who's feeling

While I feel all through
Most of it for you
I doubt you think of me
Even a percent of how much I feel for thee

On some days, I wish to
Ask you if you ever do
Think of me randomly, too
Or if it just when something pushes you to?

If even the thought of me
Runs through the mind of thee
I have no questions regarding the heart
I've known regarding that from the start

That no matter what be
It'll never love me
And somewhere I've accepted so
And embraced my sorrow

127
I loved you
Because I wanted to
But more than that is true
Is the fact that I nothing else to do

Not like I was feeling bored
Or that I had too many emotions stored
And I just needed someone to
Give it all to

In fact, if I'm true
When I fell for you
The last thing I wanted to do
Was to experience love anew

I had no intention to
Fall in love, let alone with you
And absolutely no clue
Of where this would lead us to

I still don't know where we are
So close yet so far
You tell me your deepest secrets
And I wonder if they were even secrets

For you don't seem to
Trust me like I trust you
Or maybe you do trust me
But don't know how to show it to me

Ah, classic me
Defending thee
No matter who it be
Someone else, or me

128
No matter what be
You'll never love
And while I've learnt it
I don't seem to have understood it

The implications
The complications
The questions
The tensions

The pain
The disdain
That will follow
Once all the love has flowed and left me hollow

For there'll be
No one to love you
And at the rate of how I love you
That day seems closer than you

Some nights like tonight
I think of my plight
Of what will be
When I've loved thee?

When all the love is gone
And the heart is forlorn
What will I do
With a heart that would still love you?

It might not have much to give away
For love will have flowed away
Into you, who'll never be able to see
That the love came from me

129
They ask me today
If I still love you the same way
I have nothing to say
Just like I never had anything to say

How do I say
That the way
Has changed
And yet, remains unchanged?

How do I explain
That pain
And hurt has changed
How love is arranged?

How do I prove my stance
That your ignorance
Has led me to be
Deficient of love for me?

That I can no more see
Anything other than thee
And yet I don't have the courage to say
Anything to you, even today

130
I'm scared of meeting you
Because it'll hurt me anew
How I'll see you again
And how you'll see me, again

It won't change a bit
And that'll hit
Really hard somewhere inside
And I'll have nowhere to hide

Nowhere to go
And drown my sorrow
No one to see
The storm in me

It will rage again
Tides of pain
Tears will be rain
And it'll be in vain

For the very next day
The same way
Will be repeated again
And again, and again

131
Not even miracles can change
How love does arrange
Inside my heart
Inside this broken heart

Yet, despite everything
It's no wonder I'm feeling
Love, all over again
Despite not having fully recovered from the pain

I wonder how I could
Or that if I ever would
Fall in love again
After so much pain

But look at me
Falling in love with thee
Despite knowing full well
That there'll be no story to tell

Just like my heart has you
She has her place inside of you
And while it's not okay
But somehow, adjustable in some way

I don't have an idea of how to
Control my love for you
To stop it
Or leave it

It doesn't seem to listen to me
I doubt it'll listen to thee
Maybe it's always going to be
This way with you and me

Air crackling with tension
Minds spiralling with confusion
So much heart and soul gone
And yet, left forlorn

132
I wish you were mine to be
For I am yours to be
And I will always be
No matter what be

No matter where I am
Who I am
What time it be
Love will survive me

Maybe even you
But all I want to
Is spend some time with you
Before I run out of time with you

But each time I think so
My heart fills with sorrow
Times already running out on us
And there still seems to be no existence of 'us'

It was you and me
And it still is you and me
No changes at all
Except an occasional fall

When you don't speak to me
Though you know it hurts me
It breaks me down
Turns each smile into a frown

Maybe you do
Know that I love you
That's probably why
You know you can make me cry

And you do it
Whenever you can hit
You do hit my heart
Break off another part

I wish it wasn't this way
And hope for a day
When it isn't so
And I'm not drowning in sorrow

133
Each time I tried to
Come closer to you
Tried to understand you
You pushed me away anew

And today
You taunt me this way?
That I don't know you
Though I've loved you all through?

Even though I might have loved you
I never understood you
Never knew you
And why you do what you do

Let me tell you something
That I couldn't say in such a feeling
I do know you
More than even you do

I understand you
In ways even you don't do
Because love begins there
And so does care

How else do you think
I knew it all in a blink
Of what you would need, and when
If I hadn't known you then?

But anyway
I didn't say anything today
Just like I never said anything
Just felt everything

134

I was so sure
That you were the cure
To all my pain
And would never lead to disdain

And there you were
So busy with her
Who would lead you to
All that you weren't supposed to do

While things never got there
You still do stare
Each time she walks by you
While she doesn't even seem to recognise you

I see it all
From the canteen to the main hall
Seeing you happy
Does make me happy

But that leads to think
Is it good to be swayed by a wink?
To date someone just because they look good
Or should you think if they're really good?

I'm not asking you to date me
For I know that's impossible for thee
And maybe even impossible for me
Even though I love thee

While it hurts me
To see thee
In the arms of someone else
At least you're happy, my heart tells

And somehow that seems to be enough
To deal with all the stuff
All the pain and disdain
That I suffer in your love, in vain

135
For a while, I thought of you
Never realising when I fell in love with you
I didn't even see
When love was all that was in me

And you were the one who
I gave it all to
While I felt empty on some days
I felt happier than ever in some ways

And for a while, I told me
That you loved me
Maybe you did
But you hid

You didn't want to break it to me
And I couldn't say it to thee
The air was heavy with silence
And hearts filled with violence

I went to sleep each night
Thinking of the plight
Of not being able to tell you
Telling myself that tomorrow I will do

And then came a tomorrow
Where began my sorrow
For you told me
That you loved 'she'

I hadn't even told you
That I loved you
And you broke my heart
Into a million part

It seemed like the end of the world to me
For what was even in me
Other than love for you
And the wish to be loved by you?

136

I wish there was a way
To circumvent that day
When I first met you
And spoke to you

We spoke so much
That somewhere it did touch
The inside of my heart
Which now lies broken apart

I wish this love had never begun
This pain wouldn't have been spun
There would be no need to
Ask myself the same questions anew

If I'm good enough for you
If I'm match enough for you
If I would be able to
Be the one for you

And to sleep again
With nothing but pain
Just more questions again
And no answers, yet again

And this is what goes on and on
Which makes me forlorn
For no matter how hard I try
I'm bound to fail and cry

For I know you'll never love me
No matter what be
Not because you hate me
But because you can't ever see me

The way you'd need to
To fall for me, too
And while I've made peace with it
It does hurt when it does hit

137

Not just did I love you
I even worshipped you
Everything I did was for you
Every one of my breaths was for you

And what did you do
To all my love for you
To me, who loved you
And never asked for anything from you?

Now I see
You telling her that love wasn't fair to thee
That she didn't love you just as much
That she felt like a foreign touch

That you wanted unconditional love
And hers was but conditional love
And you couldn't stand conditions in love
That if it wasn't unconditional, it wasn't love

And when I did love you
Just as you described all through
Remember what you did to me?
Remember how you hurt me?

Maybe you don't
I still hope you won't
For I will never intend to hurt you
As you've hurt me all through

138
I tried so hard to be
The way you wanted 'the one' to be
I tried to chisel myself into 'the one'
And only ended up being undone

Now I no more know
What to even do with my woe
And where it comes from anymore
All I know is that it hurts to the core

I don't know what hurts me
Losing myself to the tries for thee
Or still not being able to be
'The one' for thee

I have no clue
As what's been hurting me all through
And when I don't know
What cure can even follow?

I don't know whether to keep chiselling myself
Or to stop and learn again to be my original self
I don't know what to do
All I know is that I love you

And somewhere that adds to the pain
That I wonder if I'm suffering in vain
Or if there's even anything that's going to come out of it
Or if it's just another seasonal thunderstorm that hit

139
I wish I knew
What to say to you
That wouldn't be wrong
And would make our bond strong

Honestly, I've lost all hope
That there's even a scope
Of you loving me
Even though I love thee

I know it's not to be
For we simply can't be
We wouldn't be able to
Make it through

Why add to the heartache
Especially when there's so much at stake?
I've accepted it with pain
Which keeps coming back again and again

But a friendship can definitely be
Where love can never be
Maybe I can be a friend to thee
If not the beloved I intended to be

140
I might have loved you
I may still do
But I do know
My love isn't to show

For I know you
And that you'll never love me, too
And while that hurts on some days
At least I know you're mine in some ways

You might not be the one who loves me
But at least you're the one who guides me
Who is there to help me
When I need thee

Who would respond to my calls
Who would lead me through scary halls
Who would make me smile again
When I break down in pain

While I'm sure
That it'll never be a cure
For you'll not know why there is pain
At least I know you'll be there for me, again

And love might be there
But nothing can't replace the care
That you've given me
While not loving me

141
It's funny how
I did allow
Myself to fall for you
Even though I knew you

And that there'd never be
A forever for me
For I wonder how long do I even have with you
And what can we do

What I want from you
Is not love for me, too
But lots of memories
And a heartful of stories

Stories that I take with me
When it's time to be
Separated from you
And go away as we'll have to

Maybe we'll meet again someday
And on that day
We'll speak of today
When it's gone away

I'm sure that day will surely be
And that I'll no more be in love with thee
You'll actually be just a friend to be
Like I've been saying all this while to thee

142
I don't know why
Each night I do cry
If it's because I couldn't be her
Or because you never loved me as you loved her

And that you'll never do
No matter what I do
For I'll never be able to be
What she was to thee

It's impossible to replace someone
And it's simply not done
I can't be her in each way
No matter how hard I try each day

Because we're not the same
And trying to be the same
Would only be a mistake
With myself as stake

I've already lost both ways
Tried so hard for a number of days
That I lost me
And yet, never got to being loved by thee

Maybe that was what I was to learn
To not be what you did yearn
To be who you needed
Maybe that was the advice I needed

But for what it's worth
It's now under the Earth
Over and done, as far as I see
But, thank you for teaching me

143

Tonight makes me want a day
When you love me the same way
As I love you each day
And that the love does stay

But then, I do know why
You can't do so, no matter how much you try
You're still so much in love with her
That no one else can make your heart stir

I wonder if it's her who you love
Or who you were when you were with her, whom you love
If you miss her
Or the person you were when you were with her

I wish I could ask you
But I don't think I could do
I don't think I'd be able to
Take the answers from you

My heart is too weak to bear so
And also too filled with sorrow
That one more day has passed away
And you still won't love me the same way

But how do I tell the heart
That there's no story to start
You're never going to be mine to call
That we're separated by an invisible wall

We might be friends or so
But never will the sorrow
In either of our hearts, go away
Never will there be that 'hoped for' day

144
You've started asking about me
Speaking to me
Once again
When I finally healed from the pain

And while I try not to
I still do speak to you
For you were, in no way
Responsible for the pain, anyway

It was my expectations of you
Unrealistic all through
I wanted you to love me, too
Never realising what that'd mean for you

Never saw why
You couldn't try
For you were too busy healing
From a wounded heart still feeling

And it is now I understand
When it's the same place where I stand
You did to me
What she did to thee

Only that hers was intentional
And yours was unintentional
Maybe even unknown to you
That I'd suffered the same, too

Maybe that was what I needed to
Finally understand you
In ways I'd never known to
Even though I'd always loved you

145
It's tough to
Stay away from you
Not speak to you
Even though I want to

And on some days
The urge overpowers my ways
Of staying away from you
To heal myself all through

To kill all those feelings
And emotional dealings
That I have with you
And those I've had with you

But in some or the other way
You find a way
To come back in my life
And reintroduce the strife

I don't blame you
For you don't know it, too
The effect you have on me
The painful glee

Some days, I wish you knew
But then, I'd lose you
And that's the last thing I want to do
At least when I'm still in love with you

146
I looked for you again
Even thought in vain
Even thought I should not
Why did I do so was the afterthought

Honestly, I have no clue
I no more feel for you
Or at least that's what I say
To myself each day

Even though I know
There's still some woe
For we left an amazing story
As just a story

For someone to imagine and tell
When it was ours to tell
Ours to live through
Ours to love through

And we let it go away
Each single day
Some or the other way
We never found a way

Your pining for her
And my trying to be her
Maybe that's where
We lost our love's share

No wonder I still mourn it
And everything seems to remind me of it
I wonder if I looked for you now as a habit
Or because there's still some life to it

147
I wonder why I still try to be
The one for thee
When, according to me
I've gotten over thee

There are supposed to be
No feelings in me for thee
And maybe no feelings at all
Considering how much it pained to fall

To fall in love with you
All through
And not have you love me
Even though I tried hard to be the one for thee

They tell me
Advise me
I shouldn't try
For love has no what and no why

But they don't know
The feeling of this woe
Of going on loving someone
When you know you can never be 'the one'

148
I wish there was a way
That I could convey
Everything I wanted to say
I wish I could just say it some day

But each time I try to
Say it to you
Words fail to form
And my heart gets caught in a storm

I don't know what to do
For I know you
In ways I'm not supposed to
In ways no one is supposed to

I'm not supposed to know
What makes you feel low
What keeps you up at night
What motivates you in the daylight

I'm not supposed to know your secrets, too
Which you told me all through
Maybe they don't mean so much to you
But they mean everything to me, and they will always do

But then, when it comes to me
There can never seem to be
The right word to say
To give it all away

Or maybe it's already there
But so is the scare
That I'll lose you
When I confess to you

149
There must be something
That you're feeling
Regarding me
Given I feel so much regarding thee

It's hard to say
What to feel today
But it's pretty simple to say
That you won't love me, even today

Some days, it's hard to love you
For I know I'll never receive the same, too
But each time I throw it all away
I realise I've never known life any other way

I've never known what it is to not love
To not constantly be in love
To not look for you
To not wait for you

I've tried hard to
Let go of this love for you
But some or the other way
It finds its way back the very next day

I've stopped fighting it
For I'm never going to win against it
All I'd ever do
Is harm myself for you

And that's the last thing I'd want to do
Especially after all I've been through
There's already a lot of damage here
And the only things I need now are love and care

150
I wish I could say goodbye
Each time I said hi
I wish I could walk away
Just like you did everyday

I wish there was something else I could do
Instead of being hopelessly in love with you
I wish there was more to life
Than this constant strife

I wish I could be her
So you'd love me like you love her
I wish I could be someone else
For I'm tired of crying out entire wells

I wish nights didn't hurt so much
When each dream felt so real to touch
I wish days didn't pain so much
When each truth hurt so much

I wish there was a way
To change things just for today
For me, even just a single day
Would change things in a huge way

For I'm tired of all this today
Tired of being melancholic each day
Tired of the way it's going on each day
Tired of the way I'm hurting in each way

151
You tell me
I need therapy
How funny it is to say
It's because of you I'm this way

I've been starving for love
Waiting for love
And yet, none of it ever comes my way
And today's just another such day

On some days, you speak to me
Others, you ignore me
Forget that I exist at all
Leave me alone in silence's dark hall

For my mind to think away
Day after day
Hours go by
And all I do is cry

Cry for what never was
For love that wasn't a sufficient cause
To loved back the same by you
For you never saw me as I saw you

Some days, there's a hope in me
That, things will finally change for me
That you'll come around today
And maybe at least be kind to me today

But then, that's there about hope
The answer's always a nope
Just like it's always been
Just like I've always seen

Nothing new for me
Yet, it hurts me
So much that it hurts to breathe, too
Everything in this world, and especially you

152

I was a rose
In the hands of those
Who did not intend to
Keep me all through

I tried hard to be
What they wanted me to be
Exactly how they demanded of me
Because I felt that was glee

But it was not, and it will never be
That's a lesson I learnt from thee
The others might have just thrown me
But it was you who even crushed me

Ended me once completely
Only to allow me
To see what I'd always been
To see what everyone else had always seen

It wasn't easy
But worthy
Worth each minute of pain
If needed, I'd go through it again

It wasn't what I wanted
But what I desperately needed
The ability to know myself
And to value and love myself

I wouldn't say I was lucky
Neither do I consider myself unlucky
For all I lose and all I gained
It was worth each moment that pained

153
Some days I wish, others I pray
For a beautiful day
But then, a question comes my way
What do I lack today?

There seems to be
No answer for me
The question stays
As it has, for days

Sometimes I seem to
Find that answer in you
But then, I tell myself again
Regarding all that pain

I've known it's tough to
Get over that love for you
Get over losing you
When I never had you

And maybe that's why
I do not want to cry
At least, not again
After all those nights I cried in pain

You ask me why I'm scared of love
I wish I could tell thee, it's not about love
It's about what happens after
The way it's been months I've heard my own laughter

I'm scared of falling again
And bearing all that pain
That's why, no matter what be
I'll try not to fall in love again with thee

154

It's a new day
Yet, an old day
For all that happens today
Has happened day after day

And there seems to be
No end to this routine for me
No breaks in between
Just a dull dim sheen

No end to this pain
That seems to be in vain
That seems to do nothing
Except keep me in a melancholic feeling

Yet, in some way
It gives meaning to my day
At least something out of the mundane
Something that leaves a stain

On my heart
And each soul part
It's something new
Something out of the blue

I wouldn't say I enjoy it
Neither do I detest it
It's something that I've been through
And have accepted all through

Maybe that's about love
Not receiving the same love
It makes you feel comfortable
In a place that no one should be comfortable

155
In the midst of all this madness
I've grown to love this sadness
It's become comfortable to me
The way you could never be

Even though I wanted so
All I was met with was sorrow
Just no and never, from you
Was what I loved you through

Yet, here I am, in front of you
Saddened by you
Broken for you
But still loving you

Some nights, as I lay in bed
A question pops up in my head
Why do I still love you
After all I've been through?

Why do I love you
When I know you'll never do?
When there's nothing that'll ever be
Except more and more pain for me

Maybe it's the sadness now
That it does allow
The comfort of at least someone being there
At least in sadness, if not in love and care

156

It's funny how
I did allow
Myself to fall for you again
Despite having known the pain

Despite knowing full well
I jumped into an endless well
A path that has no way back
Just a huge pain stack

That comes in waves
Where there's no one who saves
No one there
To even care

I've drowned before
Maybe even more
And I know I'll come out of it
No matter how difficult be it

Yet, somewhere in me
I don't want to be
The one who falls again
The one who goes through pain

I wouldn't say love is all pain
But what do I have but pain?
For I love someone who'll never even think of me
Though all I think of is thee

157
It hurts me
To love thee
And to have no way
To change that today

It hurts to know
That it'll make me feel low
It hurts to be there for you
And never find you there for me, too

It pains to see
You avoid me
It pains to see
You detest me

I wonder why it is so
What did I do that made you so?
Just a couple of days back
I thought you had my back

Even though you never loved me
At least you cared about me
Even the thought had me smile
Never realised it was just for a while

Am I so bad, so incomplete? That my love so complete
Has never been enough for thee
To even care for me

158
You were my home
Away from home
My safe place
My point of solace

I thought I could tell you
All that I'd been through
That I could finally be me
In front of thee

How sad it is to realise
It was just lies
You never were there
Never did care

Never cared for me
Never saw me
As even a child who needed care
Forget someone who wanted to show you their soul bare

You didn't even treat me
The way even a beggar would be treated by me
Not even kindness was there
In each time you did stare

I wish I hadn't met you
I wouldn't have fallen for you
Wouldn't have been through
All that I had to go through

159
It wasn't thee
But me
Who was wrong
Who'd been wrong all along

It was wrong of me to
Fall in love with you
To have cared for you
More than you'd ever do

To have stayed up late
So you wouldn't have to wait
To kill my sleep to comfort you
So you wouldn't go to bed with tears anew

To walk an extra mile
Just to see your smile
To try my best to
Be there for you

To have done
All that could be done
To have lost my own self
To connect the lost pieces of thyself

Yes, I was wrong
I'd been wrong all along
For love is wrong, according to you
And all I did was love you all through

160
Worked all through
To be good enough for you
Only to see
You weren't good enough for me

And even though I see
I don't feel so about thee
You're enough for me
More than anything else will ever be

Yet, you don't see
How much I love thee
How much I care
How much love is in here

You have no clue
How much I love you
Even I don't know exactly
How much I love thee

All I know today
Is I love you more than yesterday
And less than tomorrow
And lesser than the days to follow

161
I don't even know what to say
To you today
There's so much to say
Yet, no words form today

It feels so blank today
In each and every way
Maybe yesterday is still here
When it shouldn't be here

It shouldn't be
Still hurting me
It shouldn't pain
All in vain

Yet, it somehow does so
It does bring me sorrow
Even silence pains today
Forget about how words hurt all the way

You've been avoiding me
Been despising me
I can see
Even though you hide it from me

Your silence speaks to me
Things that'd never be said by thee
It tells me things
That hide feelings

And yet, if I ask you
All I'd get from you
Is either silence or that it's not so
Even know it's been so

I'd believe you
Even though I know you
Yet, love would win again
And the truth would go in vain

162

I admit I misunderstood you
And I'm sorry, too
But can you blame me
For assuming you were avoiding me?

You've done it time and again
With a cause or just in vain
Spoken over me
Unheard me

Ignored me
Despised me
Made faces when I walked in
Shifted away when I walked in

Tried everything to
Create the most distance between me and you
And if I assumed it to be
How wrong was it for me?

I know it wasn't right to
Assume what I didn't know all through
But I don't think it was wrong to
Assume you did what you always do

Nevertheless, I'm sorry for the same
Whether or not I am to blame
I don't think it would be wrong to
Say a simple sorry to you

163
I wouldn't say
I didn't think of you today
In fact, you were all I thought of all day
Especially on a day as today

I couldn't stop thinking about you
About all we've been through
All we've spoken about all these days
All we've confessed in weird ways

I couldn't stop thinking of the time
When we'd lost count of time
When I had had no clue
That I'd love you

Now that I do
I hate to see you suffer anew
Although a different way
Yet, it hurts, today

I know you're at fault
Yet, pain is default
It hurts me
To even think of thee

Even though I don't love you anymore
But it hurts to the core
To see you suffer so
Does bring me sorrow

I wish I could take on that pain
Just once again
Not because I love you
But because I did love you

And somewhere in me
Is still a place for thee
And no matter what be
It'll always have thee

164
When I think of you
I wish to see you
And when I wish to see you
I realise why I can't see you

Why I can't meet you
Why I can't hear you
Why it's impossible to
Be with you

Why I can't take on your pain
Even though it is in vain
It is because you were casual about it
Are you going through it

And yet, somewhere
I wonder why I do care
Even when I know
All you've made me feel is low

And all I've done
Is tried to shun
The feelings that I have for you
The feelings I've had all through

Tried to kill them
By strangulating them
Yet, they've somehow managed to
Stay the same all through

I don't know
If I love you now
But what I've known all through
Is that I've cared for you like I never do

And there's nothing that can change that
Not even your indifference can belittle that
And somewhere in me
I'm not ashamed that I loved thee

165
I do lack
The strength to survive another heart attack
Is it not tough enough
With all this stuff?

Can you not do
A simple thing I need you to do?
All I asked you to do
Was to take care of you

And now you tell me
All's not well with thee
You're not well
Do you know how that makes me go through hell?

How I want to cry
Yet, I can't cry
And no matter how much I try
I can't be beside the bed where you lie

I can't even be
Next to thee
All I can do today
Is hope you get better in some way

Was it too much to ask?
Too difficult a task?
To just take care of yourself
Was it too much to ask for myself?

I don't even know what I feel
And how I'm ever going to deal
All I know is that I want you back now
It's gone on for too long now

You need to come back now
No more time will I allow
Get well soon and come back
I don't know how long I can hold these tears back

It's okay if you never loved me
And will never love me
But I did love you
And continue to

And I can't see
Anything happen to thee
At least not till I'm here
Or anywhere

166
I'm telling you
Nothing will happen to you
Not till I'm here
Not till I can be here

I don't know how
But I can't allow
Anything to happen to you
Even if there's nothing I can do

Don't go away
Not today
Or tomorrow
Or day after tomorrow

Or any day
When I know you in some way
I can't bear to see
Anything happen to thee

Even the thought is killing me
Making me cry for thee
Don't let anything happen to yourself
If not for your own, then, myself

I've never asked for anything from you
But today I do
In return for all the love I gave you
Bring my love back safe, all through

Bring him back to me
Even if he won't love me
At least I'll love him
And that's all I want from him

Bring yourself back now
No more excuses now
Come back soon
I'll be waiting, like the farmers wait for monsoon

And trust me, I'm not going anywhere
I'll be right here
Waiting for you
Till the day I see you anew

167

Don't tell me you're feeling weak
My love isn't so bleak
Nothing will happen to you
And you know it, too

It might look like that
Or feel like that
But look inside
You'll find my heart inside

Pumping all through
All my love for you
And there's nothing that can do
Anything to a heart that has loved all through

And you have that heart
Inside of your heart
Yours might not be within me
But mine is surely with thee

And I know for sure
Love is the cure
No matter what the disease
It'll solve it all with ease

I'm telling you
Nothing will happen to you
Nothing can happen to you
Not till I love you

168
I don't know how to
Complain to you
I don't know how to say
What I want to say

How do I tell you
What I want you to do
Each time when you ask me
What can you do for me?

It's a simple thing
Love's a simple feeling
That's all I'd ever want from you
That's all I've wanted all through

Yet, no one I know has been able to
Find words to express it all through
Then, how do I go to you
And tell you I love you?

And that all that I've needed all this while
Is just a few moments worthwhile
Just a few moments with you
When you love me as I love you

169
I trusted you
More than I loved you
And every chance you got to
You broke my trust anew

It took everything
To get back that feeling
Of trust, utmost and complete
Of love that could survive every defeat

Of love that never needed to
Be reciprocated by you
Of love that was always willing to
Give love to you

Tell me why
You make me cry
Why you break my trust anew
Each chance you get to

Can you not see my love?
Or do you not value my love?
Was it only her love
That was love?

Is no other's love
Truly love?
Is no other's pain
To be considered pain?

And if it is so
Why is there sorrow
In your eyes
Each time you speak of her lies?

If it isn't so
Why do you push me into sorrow
Each time you can do
No matter what has just passed through?

170
I wonder if my dream
Stays only within the realm
Of my heart
Or does it to you go far apart?

For you have been
The dream I've seen
Being with you, being loved by you
Is all I've dreamt of all through

I wonder if the winds tell you
That I think of you
And I miss you
Or that I cried for you

When she told me
All wasn't well with thee
And all I could do
Was cry for you

For emotions got the better of me
And there was no way to speak to thee
You're not very far away
Yet there's no way you could be further away

So close you've been
So much we've seen
And yet, in you, nowhere
Has there been any care

It's surprising how
You could never allow
Anything to creep into your heart
Since the very start

171
There hasn't been a day
When I've missed you as much as today
When so hard has it been for my heart
To not just break apart

Not just the pain
But also disdain
The pain of you not being here
And the disdain of you not believing my care

You tell me
How do I deal with thee?
With all that you do
To a girl who loves you

Who's done nothing wrong
In all our time, all along
But love you with her heart
Even when her world was breaking apart

Even when it was tough to
Stay in love with you
I did it, I stayed near
No matter what the fear

And what about you?
You couldn't even trust my care for you?
You couldn't even see
Me getting worried for thee?

Was it wrong of me
To care for thee
To not be able to sleep
For the amount of tears I did weep?

Just because you were unwell
Do you realise how it made me walk through hell?
And how convenient was it for you
To not have trusted me all through?

172

Each time I speak to you
I wonder what it would be to
Be with you
Be the one loved by you

But then, it's not long
When time pulls me along
And I realise it's impossible for me
To ever be the one loved by thee

I wouldn't say I'm not good enough
Just that not made of the stuff
That you usually prefer
That's where I differ

I'm fundamentally different from you
Or the ones loved by you
And yet, somewhere, in me
Still stays a place for thee

I wonder if it would make any sense
To speak of all this nonsense
Which is inside my heart
To you, part by part

But then, reality is
That this painful bliss
Is to stay with me
As long as I stay near thee

As much as I want to get rid of the pain
I know it's in vain
To try to
Run away from you

Because my heart will pull me back
And it's the strength I lack
To face another mind-heart battle today
When both are right in their way

173

I wonder what I see
When I see thee
What I hear each time I speak to you
That makes me fall for you

Again and again
Despite the pain
I walk forward
Knowing there's nothing forward

I wonder where I've been wrong
In loving you all along
In trying to get over you
All this while through

I wonder where it is
What it is
Why it is
The way it is

For the love you talk about
And the love I know about
Are, while, the same
They're anything but same

You've gotten your beloved
And I'll never have my beloved
Which is you, and will always be
No matter what be

174

Why it is just with me
Who'll never be
Able to find
What everyone else can find

Why is it this way
And has been always this way
That I never knew
What was always known by you

Why do I never get to
See the same love in you
That I've gone on giving you
All the while I've known you

Is it me
Or thee
Which of us it is and why
Who is the reason I cry?

Each night when I go to sleep
The last thing I do is weep
For I might have it all for myself
But all I have is myself

No one to love me
No one to wait for me
No one to wait
To get worried when I'm late

No one who's there
Waiting with love and care
No one to love me back
No one to complete that lack

I have what most don't have
But I lack what they all have
They have love in their life
And I have loneliness and strife

175
While I'm happy for you
For having found love anew
Somewhere in me
I wanted it to be me

For no matter how much I cry
How hard I try
I'm unable to
Get over you

Get over the love
That taught me love
Get over the feeling
That's left me reeling

Each time I see you
I fall in love anew
And while I try
To not love you seems like a lie

There was a time
Which seems like a previous lifetime
When I thought I was finally able to
Get rid of all my love for you

But that wasn't too stay
For more than half a day
For when I saw you again
I fell in love again

And again
But in vain
For I know clearly
You'll never love me

You're not wrong
It was never me all along
I might have always been there
But never worthy of your love and care

Makes me feel like I'm not enough
Like I lack all that stuff
That a girl is supposed to have on the inside
Some nights, feelings get too heavy to hide

And it's then
When I envy these women
Who've found their love
And can happily love

For I can't do so
Without drowning in sorrow
For that's become
All that's ever going to come

176
I wonder why
I still do cry
When I know
All I need to know

Maybe because
My love couldn't be a sufficient cause
To make you love me
As I love thee

It couldn't even do
What a simple hello could do
It couldn't make you see me
The way I see thee

It couldn't do anything
Yet, it changed everything
Changed the way I look at life
Change the way I perceive strife

I'm so used to it now
That I simply allow
I don't force it away
For it gives me company through the day

And when the night falls
Running through the empty halls
Comes to me
A simple melancholy

I sit with it for some time
It teaches me through time
And then I go to sleep
After I've allowed myself to weep

That's what it means to
Be in love with you
For to love someone who never love you back
Creates a infinite lack

177

You proved to me
That you cared for me
Yet, when I needed you
I never found you

Why was it so
That you never had enough time in your trough
To give some to me
When I needed thee?

Why has it always been
That my heart has always seen
Pain and coldness from your side
Each time it wanted to confide?

Why is the way
That it is today
That I have to think so much
Before telling you anything as such?

Why do I need to
Have filters with you
When I love you
And will always do?

I'm not asking you to
Love me, too
What I'm asking of you
Is to be there for me, too

I don't think it's too much
To ask for a caring touch
Not even everyday
Just on a painful day

178
After you cut the call
I stayed in the empty hall
Reminiscing all that had been
Thinking of all that could've been

Could is a hard word
Speaks of things unheard
Things that'll never be
Things that can never be

And yet, we tend to
Believe it all through
For hope seems to be there
Even when there's no love or care

There always a hope
That will never elope
No matter how tough the facts may be
It'll always be there for me

Thinking and speculating, time went by
And I returned home after a good cry
Felt lighter than I ever did
For the walls now knew a secret I always hid

179

If only I were about to store
Just a little more
I would've been able to
Hide my love for you

But more
Can I store
Inside of my heart and core
There's no space for more

So much love is there
And so much care
That there seems to be
No more space for even me

And fake as it sounds, it's really true
I've forgotten myself in loving you
In longing for thee
Have I lost what used to be me

I have no remembrance of who she was
Or why she was the way she was
I don't know who I was when I first met you
All I know is that I love you

And I've done so for long now
More than my heart can allow
More than I've ever seen till date
More than I've been able to carry of late

Now, you tell me
What do I do of this love for thee?
For you don't want it from me
And it'll have no one else but thee

180
You were never there
Each time I needed care
Each time I needed love
You were never there, my love

I wonder if I've been wrong
All this while, all along
If loving you has been a fault
Which happened by default?

I wonder if I even should
Or if I even would
Want to tell my younger self
About the love for you in my self

I wonder if it's right to
Go on loving you
To go on emptying myself
In filling love in your self

I receive absolutely nothing
Even when I give everything
I wonder if this is love
Or just pain, my love

181
All my love for you
Has been but true
Yet, why does it still feel
Like I'm yet to heal

That love will never be
What heals me
That I need you to
Heal all through

But I know for sure
That's not the cure
For it's neither plausible
Nor possible

Neither can I speak of it
Nor will you understand it
For you have healing to do, too
And you'd never notice I'm broken, too

While that be
I'll always love thee
With each broken part
Of my damaged heart

While that'll never be
Sufficient for thee
For you never wanted me
To even love thee

And it's good to know
That you don't know
For if you knew
Maybe I'd not be able to love you

And, if not me
At least, I'd love to see thee
Heal completely
From all that broke thee

Maybe then, you'd see
The damage in me
And the pain I went through
To help you heal all through

182
I'm not sure how
I did allow
All this hurt in me
Which was given by thee

I don't know
How to let go
I've never known to
Let go of my love for you

And while I know I need to
I just can't seem to
For I know it's not good for me
To go on loving thee

It annoys thee
And hurts me
And to go on doing so
Is just an invitation for sorrow

And I feel
I need to heal
There's already so much pain
That I've suffered in vain

I don't think I need to
Go through more for you
You're happy as it is
And I need to find a way to accept this

And remove the idea that you'll ever do for me
That I've always done for thee
For I know you'll never love me
The way I've always loved thee

183
Each time I saw you
I saw my dream come true
But I was wrong
I'd be wrong all along

You weren't my dream come true
At least not the dream I saw in you
You weren't my fairy-tale
For fairytales don't make one wail

But all you did was try
And work to make my cry
I wonder where I was wrong
Where I'd been wrong all along

Why, in return for love
Did I not get love?
Why, in return for care
Did I get hurt everywhere?

Was it me
Or thee?
And how wrong have I been
In all that I've seen?

Has it been wrong of me
To have loved thee?
But that can't be
For love is sacred, at least to me

I was wrong in punishing me
When it wasn't me
But it was you
Who made me suffer all through

184
Today
While I know my way
I still stumble your way
Just to remember my yesterday

Who I used to be
When I loved thee
When I cared for you
More than I'd known to

When I gave you
All I could give you
And more than what was in me
For I was so hopelessly in love with thee

Today, when I look your way
A part of me breaks away
Goes to that young girl who bore it all
Yet, never let her smile fall

She wasn't wrong
And just so strong
And you couldn't see
Someone better than thee

So you broke her down
Replaced her smile with a frown
And she complied, too
For she was in love with you

And then, suddenly
You left me
Only for me to see
That you never loved me

I won't say it's fine

For it's not fine

But it is what it is

Mind you, I only came out stronger than even this

185
I knew this about thee
That you'd never love me
Yet, I decided to
Be in love with you

Falling in love wasn't a choice
But staying, a firm choice
Even though I knew
I wouldn't be loved the same by you

Yet, I don't know why
I wanted to try
To prove myself wrong
Regarding what I'd learnt all along

It was a war that went on
And all it did was leave me forlorn
Yet, somewhere in me
I'm glad I loved thee

I wouldn't have been able to see
What love could really do to me
For you decided to
Show me you didn't love me, too

And from not loving me
You went on to hate me
While I went on to
Love you more than I knew how to

I'd have never thought love could be
What it was with thee
Thank you for teaching me
What love could really be

186
I wonder why
No matter how hard I try
I never seem to be
Any closer to thee

The same silence is always there
No matter what else be there
No matter what Life may be like
The distance stays alike

So close yet so far
That's what you are
So close that I could run to you
And so far that I'd never do

I wish it was the other way around
I wish there was distance profound
But only between where we were
Not because you still loved her

And no matter what I be
It'll never be me
And somewhere, even I know
All I'll ever feel is low

For you'll never be able to
Love me all through
And I'll not be able to
Let go of my love for you

It's scary to see
Where it's taking me
Yet, I choose to go
It's for love, that's all I know

187

I doubt there ever will be
Any cure for me
For all this sickness
Caused by lovesickness

I'm tired of trying to be
The one loved by thee
Only to go to bed again
After having tried in vain

For you don't even see
What I do for thee
All you see in me
Is that it's not her, but me

And that's enough for you
To not love me, too
Even though she left you
And I love you

Yet, you run behind her
And look for her
But what do you do with me?
Sometimes, you don't even speak to me

And yet, I continue to
Go on loving you
It's no longer conscious for me
More like a habit for me

It happens on its own
Goes on, on its own
As if it has its own mind
And you're all that's on its mind

And maybe, that's true
While that'll never be enough for you
For all you want in me
Is to see her in me

And I'll never be able to
Be her for you
For we're not the same
And we can't be the same

188
It's tiring to see
The same happen to me
Each and every day
In some or the other way

It's hard to go through
The same all through
To feel the same pain
All over again

And I'm tired of feeling so
Of drowning in sorrow
I'm tired of not being enough
Of not being able to feel enough

For all I've tried
And all I've cried
I'm done trying
I'm done crying

All I want to know is why
You allowed me to try
To be her for you
When you knew I couldn't be, all through?

You knew well enough
It wouldn't be enough
For I could never be
The one loved by thee

It wouldn't fit me
Nor would I able to be
It simply wasn't meant to be
A shoe that'd fit me

Yet, you allowed me to
Cut my feet all through
Only to see
That the shoe wasn't meant for me

You knew beforehand, didn't you?
Why did you let me suffer all through?
If not the one who'd love me
You could at least be a friend to me

Was it wrong of me to
Fall in love with you
To go on trying to be
The one loved by thee?

189
I don't even know why
I still try
Even though I know well
It's just going to be hell

And that, inside hell
Nothing'll ever be well
And this love is the hell
I chose, knowing full well

In some ways, it hurts me
To still be able to see
Other people's love be
What my love will never be

To see theirs be requited
When mine will remain unrequited
To see them feel heaven in love
While hell forms the home of my love

I don't blame you
For not loving me, too
For I understand you
And why it's not possible for you

Yet, it's not simple for me
To go on loving thee
When all I see ahead
Is more pain and dread

Yet, I go on
With my heart forlorn
I don't know why
But, I still try

190

I don't even see
The same in thee
That I used to
When I fell for you

Yet, somehow, I still do
Feel the same for you
Your smiles still do
Make me smile, too

Your pain still makes me cry
No matter how hard I try
Your anger makes me angry
Even in the midst of the greatest glee

Your health is still my biggest concern
When it shouldn't be a concern
Being able to see thee
Still means everything to me

I wonder why
No matter how hard I try
I can't seem to be able to
Get over my love for you

I wonder why it is so
That I still drown in sorrow
When I don't need to
When I don't want to

What it is that binds me
To this love for thee
When even you don't love me back
Why do I still stay back?

191
I've tried hard to
Get over my love for you
And yet, I don't seem to
Have gotten anywhere away from you

Each moment I spend alone
I wait for a call on the phone
And hope for it to be from thee
Even though I know it'll not be

Each time I'm away from you
I hope to run into you
Somehow, somewhere
Where we're running without a care

Every moment I don't see you
I worry for you
I worry if you're alright
Or in the midst of a mental fight

I wonder why I do it all
Why I repeat it all
When I know I don't need to
And that I probably should not, too

For it's incorrect to
Go on loving you
When you don't seem to
Feel the same for me, too

192
I've tried my best to
Get over you
But I've realised this
That I can't get over this

For love has been
All I've seen
And I don't seem to have a reason to
Get over you

I know you don't love me, too
And that you'll never do
Yet, it fails to be
The reason to get over thee

I'm not sure why
But I don't want to try
Not anymore
For I'm tired to the core

I don't have any energy left
Nor any reasons left
As to why
I should try

I know it seems baseless to
Simply go on loving you
When I know for sure
Silence is what I'll endure

Not like you'll stop being my friend
Or be a lesser friend
But never will I be
A girlfriend to thee

And I don't intend to be
For my love is bigger than me
And I don't think I'll be able to
Be a good girlfriend to you

So it's best for me
To just go on loving thee
Without a pause
Without any seeming cause

193
I've waited for you
More than I knew how to
And I still do
While I don't know how to

I don't know what to say
How to pass my day
All I look forward to
Is the moment I'll see you

Be it in the sunlight
Or the moonlight
All I know today
Is that I'm tired of living this way

I need to
Find something to do
Something that makes me feel
That allows me to heal

For loving you is a losing game
And it's but lame
For me to go on playing it
When I've already lost it

But I don't know how to
Withdraw from it, too
So, I just go on
As I've always gone on

194
I wonder if you think of me
Or remember me
Remember something I did
Or a secret I initially hid

For I do
Remember each thing about you
And it seems to be
Effortless to me

Maybe that's what love does to one
Leaves us completely undone
For the person we love to
Come and redo anew

But I know to be true
That day will never be for you
You'll never come to redo me
For you'll never love me

You'll never be able to see
The mess inside me
The pain I carry with a smile
The tears I spent waiting your while

You'll never know
What you need to know
Or what I want you to
For you'll never love me, too

And while I say
It's okay
I know it's not okay
And never will it be okay

Yet, I say so
Maybe out of sorrow
Maybe out of pain
Or maybe, disdain

I don't know
Maybe I'll never know
I don't think I'd even want to
Know more than I already do

For knowledge is pain
I suffer in vain
And I'm tired of doing so
Of going on drowning in sorrow

195
I wish I knew how to
Fall out of love, too
The way I knew how to
Fall in love with you

I know it's not simple
But neither was love simple
And I'm tired of it now
I'd like to be someone else now

Not the girl who wakes up to
Being endlessly in love with you
And knowing it to be true
That you'd never love her, too

Not the girl who spent her night
Crying on your plight
And woke up the next morning
Still mourning

Not the girl who broke down
Yet, hid her frown
All because she wanted you to be
Endlessly and beautifully happy

I'm tired of living that way
I'd like to be someone else today
And I wish I knew how to
For I feel like I really need to

196

Each time I know
My tears flow
For seeing you
Only hurts me anew

Reminds me again
Of the pain
That I suffer silently
When my heart breaks violently

Each night, as I lie to sleep
The last thing I do is to weep
For everything around me
Reminds me that you don't love me

And it's heavy to bear
To give love and care
And know for a fact
That it's a one-sided pact

It hurts to be
In love with thee
And yet, I don't know why
I still do, no matter how much I cry

Maybe I don't know how to
Live other than being in love with you
While that may be true
I wish you loved me, too

I wish, I really do
But I know you, too
I know you'd never love me
No matter what be

197

Some days, I wish I'd never known you
I'd never have been hurt anew
Never had known pain
And suffered in vain

Never had to be silent
When my heart was violent
Never had to see
Myself breaking down for thee

And yet, today
I see it each day
And no matter how hard I try
I do break down and cry

It's hard not to
When I know you'll never love me, too
You don't even consider me a friend
I can't even think of girlfriend

All I'd ever needed was
Not to feel like a lost cause
Which I surely do
In my love for you

198
I wish you knew
How I get affected by you
Maybe you'd see
How you should treat me

A little care
Here and there
Won't hurt you, will it?
But I'll live my life on it

You have no idea how
You've become my everything somehow
Neither do I know why
I still try

I still try to be
The one loved by thee
When I know clearly
It can never be me

And it's not wrong on your part
Neither is it wrong on my part
All I can say
Is that it hurts too much today

It hurts to be
She who is me
It hurts to see
What has become of me

Maybe just for a day or two
I'd like to be someone anew
Someone who was in love with life
Not she who was drowning in strife

199
I wish there was a way
In which I could say
All I wanted to
I wish I could tell you

What you mean to me
And how it's been for me
To have you in my heart
From the very start

I wonder if I know her anymore
The girl who didn't love you from the core
I wonder if she's still there
Wandering in me somewhere

For I never hear from her anymore
Nor do I recognise her anymore
So important you've become to me
That you're a part of me

I wouldn't be who I was
Without you as a cause
And I suppose I should thank you
For all you made me go through

While there was a lot of pain
It certainly wasn't in vain
It did make me
Who I needed to be

I'm kinder than I was
More caring than I was
And maybe I'd never have been
Such one-sided love, had I'd never seen

200
For a while, I knew
That you loved me, too
Alas, I was wrong
Yet, I loved you all along

Not like I didn't want to
But I wanted to be loved, too
And now, it feels scary to
Go on loving you

Some nights, I find myself
Crying over your self
Weeping like I never did
Hiding pain like I never hid

For what do I even say
Why do I cry today?
Everything else was perfect today
Except that you weren't kind to me today

Maybe, you had your reason to
And I've already forgiven you
I don't hold it against you
Never had I done so, never will I do

Yet, when I look back today
I see I've come a long way
The girl I used to be
Is barely a part of me

And I wouldn't say
I hate who I am today
I'm sure I've learnt a lot, too
While I suffered in my love for you

201
You were toxic for me
In ways unknown to me
And now when I see
I see all the damage in me

The damage you did
And I beautifully hid
In the name of love
In the beauty of love

I never saw you
I just loved you
Never observed what you did
Just let love do what it did

It was scary to
Go on loving you
When I knew you
For you would never love me, too

What I didn't know about thee
Was that you'd hate me
All because I loved you
More than I knew how to

I wonder how
I did allow
So much to happen to me
Without complaining to thee

I understand I never saw it was you
But at least I knew
That this was somewhere connected to you
In ways I never knew

But at the end of the day
I'm glad you've gone your own way
And that you're happy there
And that I've been happy here

I've moved on
My heart is no longer forlorn
And while everything has happened between then and today
I'd never wish you ill, not even today

It would be a lie
To say this is goodbye
For I've loved you once and it's been true
So, somewhere in me will always be you